# Di and Vi

**Amelia Bullmore** studied Dr[...]
Having started out as an actres[...]
professionally in 1994. Her first [...]
extended sell-out run at the Bush Theatre in April 2005 and
a successful national tour in 2006. It was also co-winner of
the Susan Smith Blackburn Prize and shortlisted for the
What's On Best New Comedy Award. Other plays include
an adaptation of Ibsen's *Ghosts* (The Gate Theatre, 2009)
and *Di and Viv and Rose* (Hampstead Downstairs, 2011). For
television Amelia has written episodes of *This Life*, series 2
(Writers Guild Best Television Drama), *Attachments* and *Scott
and Bailey*, series 2 and 3. She devised and co-wrote a series
of ten-minute films, *Black Cab*. She was a Denis Potter Award
finalist in 2000 for her screenplay *The Middle*. Radio writing
includes four series of *Craven*, a *Fact to Fiction*, *Cashflow* and the
afternoon plays *The Middle*, *Family Tree* and *The Bat Man*.

**Amelia Bullmore**

# Di and Viv and Rose

B L O O M S B U R Y

LONDON · NEW DELHI · NEW YORK · SYDNEY

**Bloomsbury Methuen Drama**

An imprint of Bloomsbury Publishing Plc

50 Bedford Square                       1385 Broadway
London                                  New York
WC1B 3DP                                NY 10018
UK                                      USA

**www.bloomsbury.com**

**Bloomsbury is a registered trade mark of Bloomsbury Publishing Plc**

First published 2011
Published in a new edition 2013
Reprinted 2013 (twice)

**British Library Cataloguing-in-Publication Data**
A catalogue record for this book is available from the British Library.

ISBN: PB:    978-1-4725-0857-7
      ePDF: 978-1-4725-1431-8
      ePub: 978-1-4725-0792-1

Typeset by Country Setting, Kingsdown, Kent CT14 8ES
Printed and bound in Great Britain

# Di and Viv and Rose

*For Mum and Dad*

*Di and Viv and Rose* was first presented at the Hampstead Downstairs, supported by the Peter Wolff Trust, in September 2011 with the following cast and creative team:

**Rose**          Claudie Blakley
**Di**            Tamzin Outhwaite
**Viv**           Nicola Walker

*Director*   Anna Mackmin
*Designer*   Paul Wills
*Lighting Designer*   Jason Taylor
*Sound Designer*   Simon Baker
*Choreographer*   Scarlett Mackmin
*Casting*   Sarah Bird
*Co-Producer*   Celia Atkin

It was subsequently revived at the Hampstead's Main Stage on 28 January 2013, with the following cast and creative team:

**Rose**          Anna Maxwell Martin
**Di**            Tamzin Outhwaite
**Viv**           Gina Mckee

*Director*   Anna Mackmin
*Designer*   Paul Wills
*Lighting Designer*   Jason Taylor
*Composer*   Paul Englishby
*Sound Designer*   Simon Baker
*Casting*   Sarah Bird
*Choreographer*   Scarlett Mackmin

## Act One

### Scene One

*October 1983. Lights up on* **Rose**, *raggy bow in her hair, on a payphone.*

**Rose**  Hello, Charlie, it's Rose! Guess where I am? I'm in my hall of residence! – No, there's a phone in the corridor. All the flats share it.

*Viv appears, wearing 1940s clothes. She waits, unseen, for* **Rose** *to finish with the phone. She turns a ten-pence piece in her hand.*

**Rose**  Mum's just set off and she said to say to you she expects to be home by about ten. – I know, well it's a long way from our little village. – I Have Travelled To *The North*! – No, not too bad. – We stopped halfway so she could have a nap but she seemed pretty alert. – No, it's a tiny room but it's my room! At university! – The only thing is the flat's really ugly. The walls are painted breeze blocks! – I know. And there's no window in the kitchen! There's a big poster about chip-pan fires and a blanket to put yourself out with if needs be. And a telly! I know! Why would you want a telly in the kitchen?

**Viv**  It's a microwave.

*Rose turns and sees* **Viv**, *waiting.*

**Rose**  Sorry?

**Viv**  It's not a telly. It's a microwave. An electronic oven.

**Rose**  Oh. (*Back to Charlie.*) Apparently it's a microwave. – An electronic oven.

**Viv**  Are you going to be long?

**Rose**  No. Oh. You haven't got a spare ten p, have you?

**Viv**  No.

*Blackout.*

*Lights up on* **Di**, *cap perched far back on her head.* **Rose** *appears.*

**Rose**    Hello! We live in the same flat. I'm Rose.

**Di**    I'm Di. Hello.

**Rose**    I've just been to the shop. It's useless. The carrots are bendy, the potatoes are green. I said to the shopkeeper, 'Have you got any proper vegetables?' It's the student shop! They should sell proper things!

**Di**    It's expensive as well.

**Rose**    I know. But it's full of boys. Have you ever seen as many? Honestly, it's like − you know the first time you go to France or Spain on holiday and you see a whole field of just sunflowers and you can't believe it?

**Di**    I've never been abroad.

**Rose**    Well, when you do, honestly, it's absolutely amazing. And that's what this is like except boys. Fields of boys. Don't you love it?

**Di**    I'm gay.

**Rose**    Oh, that's great!

*Blackout.*

*Lights up on* **Viv** *and* **Di**. **Viv** *pushes a bike. They chat as they cross.*

**Viv**    I can't live with these people.

**Di**    It's only for a year.

**Viv**    Did you hear about the heroic stand against apartheid?

**Di**    No.

**Viv**    There's a lad down the corridor. Last night, he went and threw a can of white paint over Barclays Bank − by the crappy student shop. Ten minutes later, police are on his doorstep. He's flabbergasted.

**Di**    Security camera?

**Viv**    White footprints all the way back to his front door.

*Blackout.*

*Lights up on* **Rose**, *pushing her bike.* **Di** *appears.*

**Rose**    Di! Look!

*She takes a bunch of coriander from her bike basket.*

**Di**    What is it?

**Rose**    Smell it.

*She squeezes a leaf and holds her fingers under* **Di**'*s nose.*

**Di**    Weird. What is it?

**Rose**    Coriander.

**Di**    What is it?

**Rose**    A herb.

**Di**    You eat it?

**Rose**    Yes. I found the Indian market. It's amazing. Can I cook you supper tonight?

**Di**    Will that be in it?

**Rose**    On it.

*Blackout.*

*Lights up on* **Rose**, *on the payphone.*

**Rose**    Hello Charlie! – Fine, thank you. – How's Mum? – Oh well, give her a kiss when she wakes up. – The course is fine. We've had to buy tons of books. They're so expensive. – Art history books especially are because of the pictures.

**Viv** *appears, with a ten-pence piece in her hand, as before. She watches* **Rose**, *as before.*

**Rose**    Oh. Well. Not so good. Honestly Charlie, they're all peculiar. There's one girl. A dentist student. Dental student. Once a week, she goes to Asda, which is a supermarket, and she buys a pack of cheese, and she cuts it into seven pieces, and she wraps them up in cling film and she writes Monday,

Tuesday, Wednesday, Thursday, Friday, Saturday, Sunday on them! There's one girl in the flat who's nice. Di. I tell you something amazing. There's a girl in the flat next door who dresses like it's the war.

**Viv**   Are you going to be long?

**Rose** *turns and sees* **Viv**.

**Rose**   Oh. Hello. I think it looks brilliant, by the way. (*Back to Charlie.*) Guess what? The girl who dresses like it's the war's standing right beside me. Waiting for the phone. – Quite, mustn't hog it, better let Mrs Miniver have a go. Bye, Charlie. Bye.

*She puts the phone down.*

All yours.

*Blackout.*

*Lights up on* **Di**, *on the payphone.*

**Di**   Thanks for the parcel, Mum. It came today. – I had a bit just now with a cuppa. Excellent. And one of my flatmates – she's really into cooking – she said it was the best Dundee cake she'd ever had. – Rose. – No, I don't like the others much. – There's a girl next door who's interesting. Viv. I'm having a drink with her tonight. – The Sports Centre's excellent. I'm on the hockey team, the netball team and the soccer team. – Yep. Lots of boys about.

**Rose** *appears, with bike.* **Di** *waves.*

**Di**   Okay, Mum, I'll phone you Friday. Ta-ra.

**Rose**   Di! I'm cooking tonight!

**Di**   Can Viv come?

**Rose**   Of course. Who's Viv?

**Di**   Next door.

**Rose**   Oh war-time Viv! She's scary.

**Di**   She's a laugh!

**Rose**  She doesn't like me.

**Di**  She doesn't know you.

**Rose**  Why does she dress like that?

**Di**  She does Sociology.

**Rose**  Let's have Viv over then. It's channa dhal and chapatis.

*Blackout.*

*Lights up on* **Di***.* **Viv** *appears.*

**Di**  Do you fancy eating at my place before we go out? Rose is cooking.

**Viv**  The annoying one?

**Di**  She's all right.

**Viv**  What's she cooking?

**Di**  I can't say it, but it'll be good.

**Viv**  Okay. See you in a bit.

**Di**  See ya.

*Blackout.*

*Lights up on* **Viv***, holding a bottle wrapped in tissue.* **Rose** *appears.*

**Rose**  Hello!

**Viv**  I'm Viv.

**Rose**  I'm Rose.

**Viv**  I brought a bottle.

**Rose**  Thank you. I hope you found us all right.

**Viv**  Di did me a map.

**Rose**  Perfect. Come in.

*Blackout.*

*Lights up on* **Rose** *and* **Di** *(plus bike).*

**Di**    He can just buy a house? An extra house?

**Rose**    Apparently he can. Charlie says property's the thing.

**Di**    I think that would be excellent.

**Rose**    Really?

**Di**    Yeah.

**Rose**    Will you ask Viv? I would, but she doesn't like me.

**Di**    Why do you want to share a house with her?

**Rose**    She will like me. It's better if you ask. You ask.

**Di**    Do you like her?

**Rose**    I think she's what we need.

*Blackout.*

*Lights up on* **Viv** *and* **Di**, *with bikes.*

**Viv**    She's annoying.

**Di**    I like her.

**Viv**    Really annoying.

**Di**    We wouldn't have to live in each other's pockets.

**Viv**    Has the stepdad bought somewhere already?

**Di**    He's still looking.

**Viv**    What if it's a dump?

**Di**    He won't make his money back if he buys a dump, will he?

**Viv**    I'll think about it.

*Blackout.*

*Lights up on* **Rose** *on payphone.*

**Rose**    Three bedrooms is perfect, Charlie, because I've got two very good friends. Di, who I live with who does Business Studies and is very sporty and her mum makes that cake. And my other very good friend is Viv, who's extremely clever and does Sociology and dresses like it's the war and lives next door. – Yes I know we're all eighteen, Charlie, but we're very mature for our age.

*Blackout.*

## Scene Two

*Lights up on Mossbank. A living room. The back wall has a hatch (with sliding door) behind which is the kitchen. A door leads out to the stairs and a hall, though it can't be much of a hall as two familiar bikes are propped against the wall. The furnishing is cheap and sparse with touches of flair. There's a skimpy settee, two hard chairs, a standard lamp and a set of wall-mounted shelves. Mossbank is the only set in the play with dimension and detail.*

*January 1984. A bright afternoon.*

**Viv** *crouches by a new telephone on the floor. She picks it up, listens, puts it down, waits a moment, picks it up again, puts it down. She continues to check it every few moments.* **Di** *enters with a big cassette player.*

**Di**   Right. Sounds. Let's get plugged in.

**Viv**   Still not connected. Thought the guy said within the hour.

**Di**   He did.

*She perches the cassette player on the shelves, still holding the cable.*

Will it work?

*She lets the cable go. The plug dangles high above the floor.*

No, it won't.

*She takes the cassette player down, squats on the floor to plug it in.*

It's not so good for the sound but it'll have to do.

**Viv**   Stick it back up there, then.

**Di**   The plug's a mile off.

**Viv**   I've got an extension cable.

**Di**   Excellent.

**Viv** *leaves the phone and exits.*

**Di** *picks up the phone, puts it down again. She takes cassettes from a case and starts to arrange them on a shelf. Picks up the phone again, puts it down.*

**Viv** *enters with an extension cable and a toolbox.*

**Di**   Excellent.

*Front doorbell bing-bongs.* **Di** *and* **Viv** *exchange an interested look.* **Di** *goes off to answer the door.*

**Viv** *is taking the plug off the cassette player so she can slip the cable neatly behind the shelf. She will then put the plug back on, attach the extension cable, uncoil it to the socket, Blu-Tacking as she goes so the extension cable lies flush with the skirting board . . .*

**Di** *comes back in carrying a parcel.*

**Di**   Parcel from my mum.

**Viv**   Very nice.

**Di** *starts to unwrap the parcel. Front doorbell bing-bongs.*

**Di**   Non-stop, our house, isn't it?

*She goes off to answer the door.*

**Rose** (*off*)   Sorry! I forgot my keys! Hello, Di. Was that the postman? I can't believe I missed our first post! What did we get?

**Di** (*off*)   A parcel from my mum.

**Di** *and* **Rose** *enter.* **Rose** *pushes her bike, whose basket contains brown paper greengrocers' bags. She props her bike against the other two, and sets about unpacking her shopping on to the hatch as:*

**Rose**   A parcel from Mrs Di! What's in it?

**Di**   I've not opened it.

**Rose**   Hello Viv!

**Viv**   Hiya.

**Rose**   A box of tools!

**Viv**   A toolbox, yes.

**Rose**   Brilliant! It's so lovely to be home. It's really good going out because you come back. And you think, 'That's our corner, that's our phone box, that's our hedge – I'm home!' I got some veg.

*Di resumes unwrapping her parcel.* **Rose** *disappears into the kitchen and will bob in and out of view taking her packages off the hatch to store.*

**Rose**   And I got these! Look! One each!

*She has three bowls, wrapped and interleaved with white packing paper.*

Ninety-nine p for three! How can they be so cheap?

*She sets down a bowl on the hatch. It rocks and rolls like mad.*

Oh no!

*She tears the paper from the other two bowls and sets them on the hatch. All three rock and roll like mad.*

That is such a swindle!

**Viv**   Didn't you try them in the shop?

**Rose**   Of course not. They shouldn't sell bowls that don't work. That is such a swindle!

**Di**   Bad luck.

**Viv**   Did it say bowls? Was there actually a sign saying bowls?

**Rose**   I could see it was bowls!

*She stacks and upturns the bowls.*

Total waste of money.

*She disappears.* **Di** *and* **Viv** *exchange a look.* **Rose** *reappears in the hatch.*

**Rose**   There's a tin of something in here called 'Marrowfat Peas'.

**Viv**   They're mine.

**Rose**   Viv, what did you think of Conrad? My *boyfriend*.

**Viv**   He seemed okay once I got over him wearing plus fours.

**Rose**   Do you think they looked silly?

**Viv**   They are silly.

**Di** *takes a note from the parcel.*

**Di**   What's plus fours?

**Viv**   Long puffy shorts. Brown corduroy in this case.

**Di**   When did you meet him?

**Viv**   Bumped into them in the canteen. They were making a racket at the Art History table.

**Di**   Listen to this. 'Dear Diane. Just a little something to welcome you and the girls to your new home . . . '

**Rose**   Ah.

**Di**   'I know Viv does a lot of work at nights so I got her some coffee . . . '

*She fishes into the parcel and holds up a small jar of Gold Blend instant coffee granules.*

**Viv**   Proper coffee. Superb.

**Di**   'And I know Rose enjoys my Dundee cake so I've made a larger one this time . . . '

**Rose** *appears in the hatch, enchanted.*

**Di**   'And the oranges are for you when you're doing sport and need refreshment. Talk soon. Mum.'

**Rose** *darts out from the kitchen, heads for the phone.*

**Rose**   What's your number? We've got to phone Mrs Di. She's a saint.

**Viv**    We're not connected.

**Rose** *picks up the phone, listens.*

**Rose**    We are. He said within the hour. What's your phone number?

**Di**    Here. I'll do it. We've been checking every two seconds!

*She goes over and dials, as:*

**Rose**    And after that, we can give Charlie a ring to say thank you for the phone.

**Di**    Hello, Mum, it's Diane. – I'm calling from our new phone in the house. – Yes, it is. Your parcel just arrived . . .

**Rose**    And Rose would like to speak to you.

**Di**    And Rose would like to speak to you.

**Rose** *takes the phone.*

**Rose**    Hello, Mrs Di. I just wanted to thank you from the bottom of my heart for the extra large Dundee cake. It's so kind of you. I love your Dundee cake. It's delicious. Goodbye.

**Rose** *hands phone back to* **Di**.

**Di**    Hiya, Mum. – Yes. Oh. Okay. Okay. Speak soon. Thanks. Bye. Bye.

*She puts the phone down.*

She's late for choir. She says you speak beautifully.

**Rose**    Ha ha.

**Viv**    This is done.

**Di**    Great stuff.

**Rose**    Is that where that's going to go?

**Viv**    It is there, now.

**Rose**    Is it going to stay there?

**Viv**    What's your objection?

**Rose**   It looks a bit ugly.

**Viv**   It doesn't matter what it looks like. It's a functional object.

**Di**   Let's see what it sounds like. This is the radio function.

*She clicks the radio on.*

Sounds good, yeah?

**Viv**   Really good.

**Rose**   You're right. Sorry. I always want things to be beautiful. Stupid.

*She goes into the kitchen.* **Viv** *takes the bowls from the hatch to the table. She starts to roll out long thin strips of Blu-Tack. She remains busy with this task from here on.* **Di** *rummages for the perfect cassette to play.* **Rose** *appears in the hatch.*

**Rose**   How do we want to live here? I mean, we could come and go and lead separate lives. Or we could really live together. I love to cook. It would save us lots of money. What if we have a jam jar? And every week we all put in, I don't know, ten pounds, and I feed us. And if someone sees there's no milk or no toilet paper or something, they can get it with money from the jar. What do you think?

**Di**   Yeah. Yeah. I mean, it does makes sense, if you really don't mind cooking, but I suppose, you know, every day's different, isn't it? I have training some evenings.

**Viv**   We're students. We're free to eat cereal three times a day.

**Rose**   Do you want to?

**Viv**   I want to be free to if I so choose. I don't want to be hemmed in to a routine.

**Rose** *comes out from the kitchen.*

**Rose**   I don't want to hem anyone in.

**Viv**   It should evolve, how we live, not be drawn up.

**Di**   It's horrible when there's no toilet paper, though.

**Rose**   I mean, just for example, what are the things you can't do without? There must be something.

**Di**   Bread.

**Viv**   Bacon.

**Rose**   Dried apricots. All I'm saying is we could just make sure –

*She sits down.*

Oof. We could just make sure we always have those in.

*She reaches for a cushion.*

That's just practical.

*She sits on the cushion.*

Oof.

**Di**   What's up?

**Rose**   Nothing. I think I'll stand up.

**Viv**   Why can't you sit down?

**Rose**   I can. It's just a bit – The thing is, Conrad has a very big thing and it's made me rather tender in the va.

**Di** and **Viv** *erupt with laughter.*

**Viv**   Thing! Va!

**Rose**   Well, all the other words have sharp corners, which is all wrong.

**Viv**   Consonants.

**Rose**   Yes. Sharp corners. Which is all wrong. Or they sound Latin. And willy is silly and fanny is my cousin. So I just stick with thing and va.

**Di**   And Conrad's thing is very big.

**Rose**   Yes.

**Viv**   The plus fours are storage.

**Rose**    Poor Conrad. I honestly think it's as difficult for a boy to have a big thing as a small one. I mean, I like Conrad's thing – a lot – but it needs to be treated with respect. You know. No sudden changes of plan. No rushing into things. You won't tell anyone, will you? Seriously, because it's not a joke. It's his body. And I honestly think he'd wear plus fours anyway.

**Viv**    Why? What's he saying? 'I am a toff.' Why would anyone want to say that?

**Rose**    He just likes them.

**Viv** *tinkers with the bases of the bowls and Blu-Tack as she talks, crossing to fetch sticky tape from her toolbox, etc.*

**Viv**    Clothes are signifiers. We're not covered in fur any more, we don't have a uniform for the species, so every day we put on a costume to signal what we want to say about ourselves. Everything's a costume. Look at Di. Her costume says, 'I am a lesbian. I embrace the lesbian world. I'm mad for everything lesbian until such time as I go back to my mum's for Christmas.' Your costume is interesting. It's sexually enticing in the most carefully calibrated way. You appear to be wearing jeans and a T-shirt –

**Rose**    I am!

**Viv**    – with an artlessly tied bow in your hair. What you are saying is – 'Hey everyone' – by which I mean men – 'I am straight. Fancy me. I am conforming to the norm enough to not alarm you, which will therefore attract you, but I have incorporated enough of a dash of individuality to make you feel you are not making a run-of-the-mill choice – which will attract you further still.'

**Rose**    Viv. You're an intellectual.

**Viv**    I am very interested in this subject. I'm going to write great works on it.

**Rose** *looks at* **Viv***'s war-time clothes.*

**Rose**    What does your costume say, then?

**Di**   'I'm nearly at the end of my ration book but the butcher says he'll save me a pig's head.'

**Viv**   Shut up.

**Rose**   I think your costume says: 'I'm unusual. Be intrigued.' Who do you want to intrigue, Viv? What are you saying?

**Viv**   I don't know.

**Rose**   You must do.

**Viv**   Your own costume's hard.

*She sets the three bowls upright. Not a wobble.*

**Rose**   Viv. You are brilliant.

**Di**   Listen to this.

**Di** *clicks on her music.*

*The music plays.* **Di**, **Rose** *and* **Viv** *clear things away.* **Viv** *disappears.*

## Scene Three

*April 1984. Dusk. The music plays (and fades) over* **Di** *and* **Rose** *heaving an armchair from the hall into the living room. During the following they move furniture around.*

**Di**   I'm really keen on this girl. Abbi Matthews.

**Rose**   Great!

**Di**   But I don't know if she's keen on me.

**Rose**   Ask her.

**Di**   It's not that easy.

**Rose**   I've just discovered if you ask a boy to go to bed with you, he will. Maybe it's the same with girls.

**Di**   Is that what you do?

**Rose**   Yes.

*The phone rings.* **Di** *heads for it.*

**Di**   You just ask?

**Rose**   Yes.

**Di** *picks up the phone.*

**Di**   Hello? – Hiya. – Viv says when's dinner and do we want cider? Thumbs up to cider and dinner's in –

**Rose**   – half an hour.

**Di**   An hour. Okay. See ya.

*She puts phone down.*

She's just at the shop.

**Rose**   Quick. Let's do this before she gets back.

**Di**   Let's shift this out the way, then.

*They do that.*

**Rose**   Do you think it'd be better over there?

**Di**   Let's try it.

*They do that.*

**Rose**   I like that. Do you?

**Di**   Yeah. Angle it? Do you think?

**Rose**   Angle it. Definitely.

*The chair's in position.*

**Di**   That's the one.

**Rose**   Let's sit in it at the same time. We've got to both fit.

*They stand in front of the chair, hip to hip. They lower their bums, as one, until they are wedged in side by side, their heads turned towards each other. It makes them laugh.*

Tell me more about Abbi Matthews.

**Di**   She's a second-year.

**Rose**  Ooh.

**Di**  Geography student. Red hair. Looks like a pixie.

**Rose**  Does she sit on the Lesbian Table?

**Di**  Yep.

**Rose**  I've seen her. I know exactly who you mean. It's funny being so close to you, Di. I can see your freckles.

**Di**  I can see your moustache.

*They laugh. Front door slams, off.*

**Viv** (*off*)  What the hell is all this?

**Di**  Ey up. Dad's back.

**Rose** *laughs.*

**Viv** (*off*)  What the hell is all this junk?

**Rose**  Ey up. Dad's back and he's not right happy.

**Viv** *enters with her bike, scowling, clatters it against the other bikes as she talks.* **Rose** *and* **Di**, *wedged in the chair, are brimming with giggles.*

**Viv**  What's all that in the hall?

**Rose**  Charlie's friend dropped it off with the chair. He thought it might be useful.

**Viv**  We agreed to have a chair. Not a load of junk.

**Di**  The chair is excellent.

**Viv**  *What are you doing?*

**Rose**  We're stuck.

**Viv**  Does Charlie think 42 Mossbank Road is a depository for all the junk in his garage? We agreed to one chair.

**Rose**  I think the fan on a stick might be –

**Viv**  Pedestal fan.

**Rose**  Yes. I think we'll be glad of that when it's hot.

**Viv**    It will not get hot. We will never need a pedestal fan.

**Rose**    Well, the filing cabinet, then. Couldn't you do with a filing cabinet? For your great works?

**Di**    Try the chair, Viv.

**Rose** *and* **Di** *try and heave themselves out. It's hard. They giggle.*

**Viv**    For God's sake. What about the sideboard? And the corner thing?

**Di**    Could you give us a hand?

**Viv**    Ridiculous. The pair of you.

**Rose**    This is like 'The Giant Turnip'!

**Viv** *hauls* **Rose** *out.*

**Rose**    I'm free! Have a go.

**Viv**    I don't want a bloody go. I want you to phone Charlie and tell him to get his mate to drive back here and shift the junk we never agreed to. I'm Charlie's tenant. There are no special terms because you happen to be his stepdaughter.

**Rose**    We can get rid of what we don't like without telling him.

**Viv**    We need to tell him so he doesn't pull any other stunts.

**Rose**    He won't.

**Viv**    We need to set some ground rules.

**Rose**    I'll phone him after dinner.

**Viv**    Phone him now, Rose, or I will.

*Silence.* **Rose** *picks up the phone and puts it on the hatch, then walks into the kitchen as:*

**Rose**    I'm not going to let you phone him, am I, because you've come back from the library in a foul mood and you'll be bolshy with him, and do it meanly, and hurt his feelings whereas I'll do it sweetly –

*Kitchen-side, she appears in the hatch and lifts up the phone.*

– and sweetly works.

**Rose** *shuts the hatch, leaving the phone cord trailing out like a tail.*

*Silence.* **Di** *switches on a lamp.*

**Di**   You have come back from the library quite militant.

**Viv**   I've just completed an extremely good piece of work and I feel uncompromising.

**Di**   It's hard for her. She's stuck in the middle with Charlie.

**Viv**   He bosses her about and she needs to tell him no, otherwise she'll never get him off her back.

**Di**   I think you're hard on her.

*Silence.* **Di** *finds the perfect cassette. Ejects the old one.* **Viv** *sits in the chair.*

**Viv**   Comfortable.

**Di**   Listen to this.

**Rose** *opens the hatch and sets down the phone.*

**Rose**   They weren't in.

**Viv**   Try him later. And you can tell him if he wants to give us something useful, get us a washing machine.

**Di**   Shall we crack open that cider?

**Rose**   Yes.

**Di** *unwraps the bottle of cider from its paper. Holds it up, approvingly.*

**Di**   'Olde English *Vintage* Cyder.' Tray sofistikay.

**Viv**   The jam jar was healthy this morning so I thought we could stretch to it. Something smells good, Rose. What's for dinner?

**Rose**   Aubergines in the pickling style and Gujurati carrot salad.

**Viv**   I love that.

**Rose**   I know.

**Rose** *sits down, turned away from* **Viv**. **Di** *sets the phone back on the floor. She goes into the kitchen with the cider. She sets the three (now forever steady) bowls on the hatch and pours cider into each.*

**Di**   Do they really drink cider out of bowls in France?

**Rose**   Yes. In Brittany.

**Di** *hands the cider round.*

**Viv**   There's this incredible woman social historian I've been reading. I'm giving this talk on corsets. I came across some articles of hers on the microfiche in the library. I'm going to write to her. I'd like to work with her. She's based in New York. Nancy-May Fleeshman. She thinks about things the way I think about things.

**Rose**   Does she have a very bad temper?

**Viv**   Di says I'm hard on you.

**Rose**   When a person cares, they come at you hard or they come at you soft, they never just come at you normal.

**Viv**   Normally.

**Di**   Is that a saying?

**Rose**   No, but it should be because it's just so obvious. And rather boring. What's interesting is that you're keen on a second-year geography pixie called Abbi Matthews. Why don't you just ask her out?

**Di**   Because. It's complicated. Do you know who Kath is?

**Rose**   No.

**Di**   Right. You know the Lesbian Table?

**Rose**   Yes.

**Di**   There's usually a woman sat there called Kath. She's a third-year. She's very powerful.

**Rose**  Is she the one with short brown hair?

**Di**  One of the ones, yes.

**Rose**  Is she the one with small, curranty eyes, quite far apart, like a gingerbread man?

**Di**  Possibly. Anyway. She sort of owns Abbi Matthews.

**Rose**  What? Goes out with her?

**Di**  No. She goes out with another woman, but she likes Abbi Matthews around.

**Rose**  Like a court jester.

**Di**  Kind of. So Abbi Matthews is sort of guarded by Kath.

**Rose**  Like a snack she may want later, on the bus home.

**Viv**  Why does everything have to be like something with you?

**Rose**  Because as far as I can see, everything is.

**Di**  Anyway. The question is –

**Rose**  'Does Abbi Matthews like Kath?'

**Di**  Yes. And if she doesn't – and if she does like me – how can I avoid incurring the wrath of Kath?

*They think and drink.*

**Viv**  You need to offer an alternative to Kath. Kath's power is sedentary. Psychological. The perception of her power is based on the threat of exclusion. Everyone wants to be sat with Kath, right? So what you do is prowl into the canteen, fresh from sport. In your shorts. A bit sweaty. A bit grimy. Strong. Fit. Independent. The Mud-Smeared Warrior.

**Di**  The mud-smeared warrior.

**Rose**  Abbi Matthews will come in her pants.

**Viv**  Go over to the Lesbian Table. Ask her out.

**Rose**  Ask her if she'd like to sleep with you! It really works. I've been on a spree. Eight boys in three weeks.

**Viv**    God Almighty.

**Rose**    So interesting. So different.

**Di**    Bloody hell, Rose. Be careful.

**Rose**    I am. Everything's under control.

**Viv**    Don't bring them back here.

**Rose**    I don't. I'm not stupid. This is Mossbank.

*She strides to the kitchen, chest out.* **Di** *whacks on her cassette.*

*Music plays.* **Di** *and* **Viv** *clear things away.*


## Scene Four

*May 1984.* **Rose** *lies on the settee with one leg flung over the back and the other flung over the arm. The pedestal fan is trained between her bare legs. Her skirt billows.*

**Rose**    Do you think I'm going to die of cancer of the va?

**Viv** *appears holding a cup of coffee and an important-looking folder.*

**Viv**    I didn't know you were back with Conrad.

**Rose**    I'm not. It's all this revising. Makes me so horny. Conrad too. Just had a quickie in the Classical Library.

**Viv**    Did you pick up my rent cheque for Charlie?

**Rose**    Yes, I've sent them all off.

**Viv** *spots two bulging laundry bags.*

**Viv**    Haven't you been to the launderette?

**Rose**    No.

**Viv**    You said you'd go yesterday. It's your turn.

**Rose**    I know, I know. I'm sorry. I'm just about to. That file looks important.

**Viv**    It's my corset talk.

**Rose**  Oh yes! Is it today?

**Viv**  Tomorrow.

**Rose**  Are you excited?

**Viv**  I know it's good. I've sent a photocopy to Nancy-May Fleeshman, in fact. I don't know what my tutor will make of it. Or the rest of the group. I don't need their approval.

**Rose**  Will you do a bit for me?

**Viv**  Now?

**Rose**  Why not?

**Viv**  Because nobody's got any clean clothes in this house until you go to the launderette.

*Front door slams, off.*

Hiya!

**Rose**  How did you get on?!

**Di** *enters in full Mud-Smeared Warrior regalia – shorts, soiled shirt, muddy and slightly bloodied knee, dirty plimsolls. She is furious.*

**Di**  Been in and out the canteen all bloody morning. No sign of her. I must have gone in there five times. Then I ran round the campus to see if I could spot her. Which of course I didn't. Went back in again. No sign. I look like a pillock and I need to wash this fucking jam off my knee.

*She stomps into the kitchen.*

**Rose**  Oh bad luck, Di. Bad luck. You don't look like a pillock.

**Di** *starts undressing, glimpsed through the hatch as:*

**Di**  Get this kit off for a start. It's rancid. What a fucking morning. Where's the clean clothes, Rose?

**Rose**  I'm afraid I haven't been yet.

**Di**  You haven't been to the launderette?!

**Rose**    I'm just about to.

**Di**    You said you'd go yesterday! When you say you're going
to go you have to go, like we do when it's our turn and we
wash your clothes for you!

**Rose**    I'm going to go right now. Sorry.

**Di**    What have you been doing all morning?

**Rose** *winces off the settee.*

**Rose**    I had a lecture. 'Painted Pottery in Ancient Greece'.

**Di**    That was at ten. Have you been shagging?

**Rose** *hobbles into action.*

**Rose**    Yes.

**Di**    Honest to God!

**Rose**    Sorry, Di. I'm going right now.

**Di**    You can add these to the pile.

**Di** *slings the Mud-Smeared Warrior kit through the hatch.* **Rose**
*scurries to pick it up and crams it into the bulging plastic laundry bags
as* **Di** *stomps through the living room in her sports bra and pants on her
way upstairs. Once she's gone,* **Rose** *and* **Viv** *look at each other,
shocked.*

**Rose**    That's a side of Di I've never seen.

**Viv**    It took you to coax it out.

**Rose** *reaches up to a jam jar of money on the shelf by the cassette
player. She counts out ten- and fifty-pence pieces, leaving only coppers as:*

**Rose**    I'll get out quick before she comes down again. Poor
Di. I'll fold everything beautifully.

*She staggers out with the laundry.*

**Viv**    Wheel it on your bike.

**Rose**    I always drop some. I'll be fine. It's only up the road.

*Front door slams, off.* **Viv** *opens her file. Glances at a paragraph to check she's memorised it. Once she starts speaking, she can stop and check, go over things she thinks she can do better, mark the page with a pencil.*

**Viv**   'Can it be argued that female emancipation was kept in check for over three hundred years by one single, perfidious garment: the corset? Course it can. A fiendish, confining confection of fabric, leather, bone and steel to whittle the female waist away. And waste away she did. Short of breath, liable to faint, unable to exercise, the mythical Fragile Female – to the satisfaction of men, whose sense of potency was boosted by the enhanced physical polarity – became a reality. The disadvantages to Woman were outweighed by the advantages to Man – breasts were not only pushed up by the rigid stays for Man's delight, but palpitated with fetching frequency as their owner fought to fill her strangled lungs with shallow breath after shallow breath.'

**Di** *enters, wearing pyjamas.*

**Di**   What are you doing?

**Viv**   Practising my talk. Shall I do you a bit?

**Di**   No. I'm too wound up. Do you fancy a tea?

**Viv**   I'm fine.

**Di** *heads into the kitchen.*

**Di**   What is she like?

**Viv**   I know.

**Di**   I literally haven't got any clothes.

**Viv**   I'm in the same boat.

**Di**   No you're not, 'cause you won't machine-wash half of yours, which is why every time I have a bath there's a sopping wet rayon frock dripping on my head.

*She tinkers about in the kitchen.* **Viv** *silently but animatedly mouths the next paragraph of her talk.*

**Di**    She'll catch something if she carries on like this.

**Viv**    She says she's safe. It's her body.

**Di**    We should talk to her.

**Viv**    She just makes light of it.

**Di**    One of us should say something in a quiet moment. I'd hate something bad to happen to Rose.

*Doorbell rings like crazy, letterbox flaps, key rattles off.* **Rose** – *screaming, panting* – *speed-hobbles in.*

**Rose**    Abbi Matthews is in the launderette!

**Di**    You're kidding!

**Rose**    Quick! Go! She's just put thirty p in the dryer!

**Di** *starts to go, realises.*

**Di**    Look at me! I can't go!

**Rose**    You can! Say to her, 'I'm so desperate to talk to you, I've rushed here in my PJs!'

**Di**    Don't be ridiculous!

**Rose**    Borrow something of mine or Viv's.

**Di**    No! That's not me! That's you!

**Rose**    You must have something.

**Di**    No, Rose, I've got nothing, because you didn't pull your weight!

**Rose**    I'm so sorry I'm so sorry.

**Viv**    Have you really got nothing?

**Di**    Nothing. The clothes my mum got me for Freshers' Week.

**Viv**    Stick 'em on. We'll fix it.

**Rose**    Hurry, though!

**Di** *stomps off as:*

**Di**   Honest to God, Rose, I could wring your neck.

*Silence.*

**Rose**   Thing is. If it wasn't for me she wouldn't even know Abbi Matthews was in the launderette, so I think it's a bit –

**Viv**   Don't even try it.

*Silence.*

**Rose**   Have you seen the clothes from her mum?

**Viv**   No.

**Rose**   Do you really think you can fix it?

**Viv**   Depends what I've got to work with.

**Di** *enters. She's in a matching top and trousers, with sewn-on details. It is awful and unsaveable.* **Viv** *and* **Rose** *see instantly it's a disaster.* **Rose** *is almost scared. A new sense of doom has made* **Di**'s *anger deadlier.*

**Di**   Think you can fix this?

**Viv**   No.

**Di**   Good. I agree.

**Rose** *holds her hands over her face.*

**Di**   Anything to add, Rose?

**Rose** *shakes her head, no.*

**Di**   No.

*She claps her default cap on the back of her head, heads for the front door, turns, points a blaming finger.*

This is not the Mud-Smeared Warrior.

*She goes. Front door slams, off.*

**Rose**   Oh God I feel terrible. What do you think will happen?

**Viv**   I've no idea.

**Rose**   Shall I go and explain?

**Viv**   No.

**Rose**   I could tell Abbi Matthews it's my fault.

**Viv**   No.

**Rose**   What can we do?

**Viv**   Nothing. Di has to do it on her own.

**Rose**   I can't just wait here, I'll go mad.

**Viv**   You could have a look at my corset talk.

**Rose**   Oh. Er. Okay.

**Viv** *hands* **Rose** *the file.* **Rose** *starts to read, frowning. She looks up.*

**Rose**   I hope she's all right.

**Viv**   Don't stop.

**Rose** *obediently resumes reading, watched intently by* **Viv**. *After a while:*

**Rose**   Blimey, Viv, it's very – the way you put things and the words you use – it's very . . . fancy.

**Viv**   I think how you say what you say is every bit as important as what you say.

**Rose**   I mean this is amazing stuff really. Three hundred years . . .

**Viv**   What's really amazing is there was a break in that three hundred years. During the French Revolution women abandoned the corset. But then they were forced back into it.

**Rose**   By who?

**Viv**   By the manufacturers, the fashion industry, society, men!

**Rose**   But how do you force a person like that?

**Viv**   Hegemony! People don't even realise they're being led by the nose because the chains are buried so deep.

**Rose**   Who's buried the chains?

**Viv**   Society! Men! I mean, the corset changed its face over that time. Flattening plank, hourglass, long smooth elastic tube – I've made photocopies of the patterns and everything – but it's the same thing. A means of control. Because if a man can span his hands round a woman's middle, he has her. The waist is a male construct. That's what I think.

**Rose**   Do you ever think you think too much?

**Viv**   There is no situation which isn't improved by thinking.

**Rose**   Oh Viv! Thing and va!

**Viv**   What about thinking, 'Is this thing worthy of my va?'

**Rose**   I always think that and I always think yes.

**Viv**   'Is this thing likely to give me AIDS or herpes or a baby?'

**Rose**   Only boys get AIDS.

**Viv**   That is *rubbish*!

**Rose**   Well, I'm careful!

**Viv**   There's a fascinating world out there, Rose. Why don't you cross your legs and read the newspaper and learn about it?

**Rose**   I am learning. By doing.

**Viv**   You're certainly doing.

**Rose**   I am learning a lot.

**Viv**   Why not go professional?

**Rose**   What? Be a prostitute?

**Viv**   Isn't that the logical conclusion of sleeping with eight men a fortnight?

**Rose**   I choose the boys I sleep with! I've never had a nasty time and I've never done anything I didn't want to. I'm free. And I'm happy.

**Viv**    Okay. Okay. Just −

*Front door slams, off.*

Be careful.

**Di** *enters, inscrutable. She takes her cap off and spins it on to something.*

**Di**    Ten a.m. tomorrow. Swimming baths. Me and Abbi Matthews.

**Rose** *hurls herself jubilantly at* **Di**.

**Rose**    Oh Di! I'm so happy!

**Viv**    Very well done. How was it achieved?

**Di**    I made her laugh about the gear. I told her I would like to see her sometime not in a crowd. She said she'd like that too but she didn't want to upset Kath. I said, 'Fuck Kath, let's go for a swim.' And she blushed. She blushed very deeply, and it was very gorgeous and I intend to make her blush again for a different reason.

**Rose** *whoops a raunchy crescendo of approval.* **Viv** *laughs.*

**Rose**    Brilliant, Di!

**Di**    So what have you cats been up to back here?

**Rose**    Well, Viv is very cross about corsets even though none of us has to wear them. And she thinks that the female waist is something that's been invented by men.

**Di**    What?!

**Rose**    It's rubbish! You only have to look at nudes in paintings. The Rokeby Venus! She has a waist! The Birth of Venus! She has a waist! −

**Viv**    Who were they painted by? Men. The Venus de Milo has no waist! −

**Di**    I don't know who any of these birds are but it is rubbish. My dad has a waist! When he's stretched out − you know − on a picnic blanket.

**Rose**   Who do you think carved the Venus de Milo? Your granny?

**Viv**   No, most likely was carved by a man, yes, but in the pre-corset age, before the waist was – (*imposed*)

**Di**   Shut up! Rose, you've caused enough trouble today. Get back to t'launderette, wash us t'clothes, cook us t'tea.

**Rose**, *chortling, looks in the jar.*

**Di**   And you, madam, stop talking rubbish and go and polish your filing cabinet.

**Rose**   Oh no, there's nothing in the jam jar and there's nothing to eat! Poppadoms and marrowfat peas! What would Madhur Jaffrey say?

**Di**   'Get it down your neck.'

**Viv** *barks a laugh.* **Rose** *and* **Di** *exit.* **Viv** *is the last to exit and resumes practising her talk as she goes:*

**Viv**   'The digestive system of the corseted woman was so constricted that her faecal matter resembled that of a rabbit.'

*Blackout.*


## Scene Five

*February 1986. Two a.m. The funereal opening bars of Prince's 'Let's Go Crazy'. Mossbank appears to be deserted. After a few moments,* **Viv** *and* **Rose***, in coats, push their bikes in and prop them against* **Di***'s bike.* **Di***, the DJ, still in her coat, flings open the hatch to reveal herself dancing and drumming in the kitchen. As the song plays, the three switch on lamps, get their coats off, charge up the Rose bowls – everything to the beat. They know the song well. They sing and dance for themselves and for the others' entertainment. They particularly enjoy certain phrases. 'Take a look around u / At least you got friends' and 'Maybe it's cuz / We're all gonna die'.* **Di** *might do some bravado drumming on furniture with wooden spoons or cutlery.* **Viv** *and* **Rose** *love the backing vocals: 'When we do', 'What's it all for' and 'Oh no, let's go'. As the song gets* *wilder so do the antics. I'd suggest shameless use of the hatch. When the keyboard melody vamps up and down in its repeated phrase,* **Di** *and* **Viv** *and* **Rose** *might vamp up and down and on and off the settee and comfy chair. The particulars don't matter as long as they do go crazy and it feels like a spontaneous, euphoric act.*

*In a quiet moment,* **Rose** *might shout:*

**Rose**   This is such a good sound system!

**Di** *might throw herself into the closing guitar solo with particular abandon. Any of them might. When the song climaxes, they fling themselves down, wherever they are, panting. They all look up or out in different directions. A lovely calm.*

**Di**   A good night. An excellent night.

**Rose**   Did you have a good night, Viv?

**Viv**   Oh yes. Oh yes.

**Rose**   What did you love best?

**Viv**   The dancing dancing dancing. And the girls dressed as boys. And the boys dressed as girls. And the dancing.

**Di**   And the bouncer letting us jump the queue.

**Viv**   We are Mossbank. We don't queue.

**Rose**   Shall I make us a snack?

**Di**   Only if you can move.

**Rose**   I can't.

*Silence.*

**Viv**   My ears are ringing.

**Di**   Me too.

*Silence.*

**Viv**   Pantheism. Cupola. Quatrain. Effulgent. Redolent. Serpentine. Stockade.

**Di**   What's that?

**Rose**   Viv's turned.

**Viv**   It's. God knows why it's going round my head now. It's a week's worth of words. We had to learn a word a day and at Sunday tea we had to recite them.

**Di**   Why?

**Rose**   So Viv could use big words.

**Viv**   So we wouldn't be tripped up by big words. So we wouldn't look fools. That was the fear. One of them.

**Rose**   You don't like your mum and dad, do you?

**Viv**   I just don't need them.

**Rose**   We don't need anyone any more. It's like dates. You know you can survive on just dates. In the desert. You two are my dates.

**Di**   I think you need water as well.

**Rose**   Let's stay here after we've graduated. I don't want to go back to my little village and all the curtains drawn.

**Di**   What, so people can't look in?

**Rose**   No, my mum always has the curtains drawn.

**Viv**   What. The fuck. Is your mum's problem?

**Rose**   Well it's partly the pills and it's partly her. She was so sad when Dad died she had to take them. And then Charlie came along and sorted everything out. He paid her income tax and bled the radiators. I think she was so relieved she married him. It was all right. We watched an awful lot of telly. All the old films. Mum wearing dark glasses and the blind pulled down. I think Charlie's had enough. I think there's some of that bread left. Do you want some?

**Di**   Yeah.

**Rose**   Viv. Do you want some bread?

*Silence.*

Viv.

*She crawls over to **Viv**, joggles her.*

She's fast asleep.

*She smiles lovingly at **Viv**'s face.*

**Rose**   She's got her lips pressed together with all the things she won't tell us.

**Di**   She's a dark horse, our Viv.

**Rose** *wanders to the kitchen.*

**Di**   What will you do, Rose? Have you got a plan?

**Rose** (*only glimpsed in the kitchen*)   I'd like to do something where I'm surrounded by beautiful things. Maybe in an auction house. Or a museum. And I'd like to go to places full of beautiful things. Florence and Venice and Paris. I wouldn't mind being a wine-taster now I come to think of it.

**Di**   Well, that all sounds well researched.

**Rose** *appears from the kitchen with two hunks of bread. She and **Di** settle with their bowls of drink and their bread. Dunking.*

**Rose**   Gorgeous.

*She sniffs her bread.*

I think, a lot of things we like the smell of is because it smells of sex. Bread. Cheese. The seaside.

**Di**   I smelt cheese once. It was me. I've used foot powder ever since.

**Rose**   I don't mean bad cheese, I mean Emmenthal. Emmenthal smells exactly like thing.

**Di**   I'll definitely stick to va.

**Rose**   You can't deny the seaside. Rock pools are pure va.

**Di**   I'll give you rock pools.

**Rose**   I'll be all right. Won't I?

**Di**   Course you will.

**Rose**   You definitely will. Whatever you do.

*They munch/drink in silence for a bit.* **Rose** *moves to be beside* **Di**.

**Di**   Hello.

**Rose**   Hello.

**Rose** *gazes lovingly at* **Di**'*s face.*

**Di**   What's up?

**Rose**   Would you like a little kiss?

**Di**   Don't be daft.

**Rose**   I think it would be nice.

**Di**   Rose. No. Don't do big eyes at me. No.

**Rose**   Go on.

**Di**   I'm not interested.

**Rose**   Am I not your type?

**Di**   No.

**Rose**   What's your type?

**Di**   Lesbians.

**Rose**   Please.

**Di**   No.

**Rose**   Why not?

**Di**   I've said. I'm not interested. I know your sort. Time-waster. Technically inept.

**Rose**   That's outrageous!

**Di**   It's a no, Rose.

**Rose**   No. Is it really?

**Di**   Really. That's not what we are.

**Rose**   Okay. Have I offended you?

**Di**   No.

**Rose**   Have I made a fool of myself?

**Di**   No.

**Rose**   Will it be awkward in the morning?

**Di**   No. Not at all.

**Rose**   Okay. Thanks, Di. Sorry.

**Di**   I'm going to bed now. Not because you can't resist me. I understand that. But I've got a match in the morning and we need to batter them.

**Rose**   Okay.

**Di**   Come here.

**Di** *hugs* **Rose**. **Rose** *squeezes her tight, burying her head into her.*

**Di**   Keep your head tucked in, that's it. No tricks.

**Di** *peels away and heads out.*

**Rose**   Night.

**Di**   Night.

**Rose** *sits for a while. Watches* **Viv**'s *peaceful breathing.* **Rose** *throws her bread at* **Viv**'s *head.*

**Viv**   Hey! What?!

*She sits up, torn from sleep, spiky.*

What the hell did you do that for?

**Rose**   Sorry. I just want to talk to you.

**Viv**   I was asleep!

**Rose**   Shall I make you a coffee?

**Viv**   No. I just want to go to bed.

**Rose**    Please. Just for a few minutes. I'll make you a coffee.

*She heads to the kitchen.*

Have you sent Wendy-May Fleeshman any more work?

**Viv**    Nancy-May Fleeshman. Yeah.

**Rose**    Do you think she reads them?

**Viv**    I've no way of knowing.

*Silence.* **Viv** *gets herself in the comfy chair, which has become her chair.* **Rose** *appears with the coffee.*

**Rose**    I just did a really stupid thing. I tried to kiss Di.

**Viv**    You did what?

**Rose**    I know. She wasn't having any of it.

**Viv**    What were you thinking?

**Rose**    I didn't think about it.

**Viv**    Fucking hell, Rose. What is wrong with you?

**Rose**    I know it was stupid. I've said. I've said it to her and I've said it to you.

**Viv**    That's insane. What – you know – where was that supposed to lead?

**Rose**    I don't know! Don't get cross!

**Viv**    What is going to become of you?

**Rose**    What do you mean?

**Viv**    Why do you have to get everyone?

**Rose**    I don't.

**Viv**    You do. You have to have everyone. It's a compulsion. It's colonisation. You're a machine designed to coerce people into attachment. Everyone's fair game. Every shopkeeper must be charmed. Mrs Di. You'd hump a lump of stone if you thought you could get it to love you.

**Rose**   I get attached to people, that's all. Sometimes very quickly. Whether they get attached to me doesn't matter.

**Viv**   Nothing matters more to you! That's why you use kindness.

**Rose**   I don't 'use kindness'. I am kind.

**Viv**   You're not kind, you're needy. Which is why you're promiscuous. You're throwing yourself away. You'll have nothing left. You need to start saving yourself.

**Rose**   Is that what you're doing? 'Saving yourself'?

**Viv**   We're not talking about me. You have to ask yourself why you sleep with so many people.

**Rose**   Why don't you sleep with anyone?

**Viv**   I don't subscribe to the confessional school of friendship, Rose – you show me yours, I'll show you mine. It's infantile.

**Rose**   Have you ever slept with anyone?

**Viv**   I don't wish to turn out my pockets for you. And you shouldn't need me to. If you insist on liking me – like what I am, not what I've done or do.

**Rose**   What you've done and do is you. Which is why I want to know why you don't sleep with anyone. Maybe you do. Maybe you make arrangements outside Mossbank and keep them under your hat. But I don't think you do and I wonder why.

**Viv**   Because I'm busy getting myself a first-class honours degree. Which, lest we forget, is why we're here.

**Rose**   I think it's because you can't be intimate.

**Viv**   What you do isn't intimate. It's smash and grab –

**Rose**   It's a lot more intimate than thinking, thinking, thinking, which is all you do –

**Viv**   It's meaningless.

**Rose**   It is not. Listen to me. Really listen. When I find a beautiful boy. And I don't mean good-looking or anything as boring as that. I mean a boy who has a sweet mouth or good jokes or something. And when we have sex. What we do, without knowing each other, is we join up. And you go very deep with a person, very quick. You see very deep into them. I slept with a boy recently. He was very sweet during and bad-tempered afterwards. And what's interesting about that is his brother was exactly the opposite.

**Viv**   You slept with both of them.

**Rose**   Not at the same time. Weeks ago. Now. I know something about both those boys they probably don't know themselves. Another boy. A Japanese student on a cultural exchange. We drank beer in the union and we went to his room and we could barely communicate a word to each other. And afterwards. Lying with him, breathing the same, feeling the same – heavy and light and quiet – I thought, 'I wouldn't mind dying now,' because at that moment there's no separateness. I melt from my separateness into theirs and all separateness goes. Do you understand?

**Viv**   Life is separateness.

**Rose**   It's the opposite!

**Viv**   We don't ask to be born. We're not warned when we'll die. What could be more separate than that?

**Rose**   Well, if we're so separate –

**Viv**   – What you're describing is a momentary –

**Rose**   – If we're so separate –

**Viv**   – a momentary delusion that it's otherwise!

**Rose**   – If we're so separate, why does anything I do have anything to do with you? Who are you to look down from on high? It's got nothing to do with you!

**Viv**   It has!

**Rose**   Why?!

**Viv**    Because what you're doing is frantic!

**Rose**    Who are you to tell me I'm frantic? Who are you to tell me I'm not kind?

**Viv**    You use kindness to ensnare.

**Rose**    I am kind! Not to get people. Because I believe in it. It makes me happy. You should try it. Maybe if you were kind, you'd be happy.

**Viv**    You can't have everyone! *You've got to learn.*

**Rose**    I think you're jealous of me.

**Viv**    Why would I be jealous of someone so stupid?

*Silence.*

**Rose**    That was an evil thing to say.

*She exits.* **Viv** *stays. Lights fade.*


**Scene Six**

*Pitch black.* **Rose**'*s face like a moon in the dark. Every breath and swallow audible.*

**Rose**    I want to report a rape. – It's not me. It's my friend. Diane. – We're at home. It happened at home. He broke in. We didn't hear. We were asleep. – 42 Mossbank Road. – Oh – Why can't I report it for her? – I see.

*Lights fade up slowly.*

*Night.* **Viv** *leads* **Rose** *and* **Di** *in the construction of a giant bed/shelter. They drag mattresses into the living room and arrange them alongside each other on the floor.* **Viv** *positions the standard lamp, the pedestal fan and anything else tall (up-ended settee?) so that a sheet can be stretched across them to form a 'roof' above the mattress floor. Bedding and cushions are arranged on the mattresses. When the shelter is ready,* **Rose** *and* **Viv** *remove* **Di**'*s slippers and dressing gown and help her into bed.*

**Rose** *and* **Viv** *turn out all but one small light and get in either side of* **Di***. They all lie in the same direction. They go to sleep.*


## Scene Seven

**Di** *starts awake with a shout of fear and leaps from the den/bed.* **Viv** *and* **Rose** *wake, alarmed.* **Di** *is unable to stay still.*

**Di**  Agh! Agh!

**Rose**  Di. Di. It's okay.

**Viv**  Are you okay?

**Rose** *goes to hold* **Di***.* **Di** *recoils.*

**Di**  No.

**Rose**  Sorry.

**Di**  Fuck. So real. So real. I want to have another bath.

**Viv**  Come on, then.

**Rose**  Do you want to report it to the police?

**Di**  I don't know.

**Viv**  The Rape Crisis Centre's got a number you can ring twenty-four hours a day.

**Di**  No.

**Rose**  We could move out of Mossbank.

**Di**  Why didn't I stop him? Why didn't I get out of it?

**Viv**  He had a knife!

**Di**  What could I tell the police? Nothing. He smelt of cigarettes. I couldn't even see him.

**Viv**  They might get something from something he said.

**Rose**  What did he say?

**Di**   He said: 'I don't want to hurt you but I will if I have to.'
He said: 'Say you like it.' He said: 'Sorry.'

*Dissolve to:*

**Viv** *stands with her toolbox.*

**Viv**   Window locks on every window. Proper strong ones.
Mossbank is defended. What did Charlie say about the alarm?

**Rose**   He said if we get some quotes, he'll send us the
money.

*Doorbell bing-bongs. They all freeze.*

**Di**   You told them the address. I heard you.

**Rose**   They wouldn't just come, would they?

**Di**   I don't want to talk to the police.

*Doorbell bing-bongs again.* **Viv** *takes a hammer from the toolbox.*

**Di**   Don't answer it.

**Viv**   Just going to see who it is.

**Viv** *goes, wielding the hammer.*

*Dissolve to:*

*Parcel wrapping, open and empty.* **Di** *unpeels a satsuma.* **Rose** *nibbles
a flapjack.* **Viv** *licks coffee granules from her finger, dips it into her new
pot of Gold Blend, repeats.*

**Di**   'Dear Diane, Here are some treats for you and the girls.
I've tried you on the telephone a couple of times but, alas, no
luck. I expect you've been out and about. Dad's snowdrops
are "best ever" this year. Hope you're well. Mum.'

**Viv**   I like that 'alas'.

**Rose**   Mrs Di doesn't have a nasty bone in her body.

**Di**   She can bear a grudge.

**Rose**   Really? Can she?

**Di**   Oh yeah.

**Rose**  Like what?

**Di**  She's not spoken to one of her sisters for ten years.

**Rose**  Why?!

**Di**  A borrowed tent was returned in poor condition.

*Viv really laughs.*

**Rose**  No! No! Really?!

**Di**  Ten years. Not a word. I can't tell her. It'd be our first conversation about sex.

**Rose**  Would you like to go home?

**Di**  I always thought, when there's a woman I'm really steady with, I'll take her home and say, 'This is whoever. This is the person I want to be with. She's a woman.' Which'd be easier for everyone to get their head round than, 'I'm into women in general.' I don't want to go home. I just want this. I don't want the Lesbian Table to know. I don't want people to reclaim the night for me, or raise money for another women's minibus because this Business Studies third-year sleeping in her bed got –

*Silence.*

**Rose**  You could leave your course. You could do your third year again next year. Sit your exams then.

*The phone rings.*

**Di**  Don't answer it.

*Dissolve to:*

**Rose** *is dozing.* **Viv** *pushes her bike in, unpacks books and papers.*

**Viv**  Where's Di?

**Rose**  She went to the Rape Crisis Centre.

**Viv**  On her own?

**Rose**  She insisted on it.

**Viv**    That's big.

**Rose**    I know.

**Viv**    I found Di's tutor. I told her Di's been poorly. She gave me some work for her. And I went to the sports centre and told them Di's injured her leg.

**Rose**    Why did it happen to Di? Why wasn't it me or you?

**Viv**    Because she sleeps in the back bedroom.

**Rose**    Do you think, maybe – because she's gay – she might –

**Viv**    What?

**Rose**    Well – have a better chance of – getting over it?

**Viv**    Better than if she was woman who has sex with men?

**Rose**    I'm not saying, Viv, I'm just asking.

**Viv**    What if she'd known him? Better or worse? If it had happened in a park? Better or worse?

**Rose**    I don't know!

**Viv**    Every man I see out there, Rose – every single one – I want to stick something up him and make him squeal.

**Rose**    I wish it had been me.

**Viv**    Don't be daft.

**Rose**    I do. I've given up sex.

**Viv**    You haven't left the house for weeks.

**Rose**    When I do, it won't make any difference. I've given it up.

*Dissolve to:*

**Di**, *dressed, galvanised.*

**Di**    She's really easy to talk to. Her name's Elaine. She's worked at Rape Crisis since they started. She said it's not an act of sex, it's an act of violence. She said I'm not a victim, I'm a survivor. She said the only person responsible for what happened is him. He chose to do that to me. I did nothing wrong. She said I shouldn't feel duty bound to report it. He's responsible for what he does to women, not me. She said as long as I've got the sheets and what I was wearing, unwashed, which I have, I can report it any time, I've got the option. She said anything I do that helps me feel I'm getting control back is what I need to do because the guy who did it to me –

**Viv**   – the guy who raped you.

**Di**   When he did that –

**Viv**   – raped you.

**Di**   Yeah.

**Viv**   Say it, then.

**Di**   Raped me.

**Viv**   When the fucking prick who raped you, raped you –

**Di**   When the fucking prick who raped me, raped me –

**Viv**   *When the fucking prick* –

**Rose**   *– fucking prick!* –

**Di**   – She said when the fucking prick who raped me, raped me he tried to take away my power, and if I let him take away my power, then I let him rule my life!

*Dissolve to:*

**Di** *slumps in the den, alone. She looks dreadful: exhausted, beaten.*

*After a while* **Rose** *enters from the kitchen, carrying a Rose bowl.*

**Rose**   I've made some soup.

**Di**   I don't want anything.

**Rose**   You're not eating, darling.

**Di**   I can't.

**Rose**   The thing is, you need to.

**Di**   I can't.

**Rose**   Would you try just a bit?

**Di**   No.

**Rose**   A spoonful.

**Di**   Okay.

**Rose** *feeds* **Di** *a spoon of soup.*

**Di**   It doesn't taste of anything.

**Rose**   Hang on.

*She goes to the kitchen and quickly returns with some chilli sauce.*

Let's try this.

*She seasons the soup, carefully stirring the sauce in. She offers a spoonful to* **Di**. **Di** *tries it.*

**Rose**   Any better?

**Di**   No.

**Rose**   Still doesn't taste of anything?

**Di** *shakes her head, no.* **Rose** *re-seasons, liberally. Offers another spoonful.* **Di** *accepts it.*

**Rose**   Better.

**Di** *nods.* **Rose** *feeds* **Di** *with stealthy skill. Chatting away, she posts soup in, nonchalantly, from time to time, when the moment is right . . .*

**Di**   How old was your mum when your dad died?

**Rose**   Well, she's fifty-two now and I was nine when he died and I'm nearly twenty now so she must have been. Um. What would that be. Fifty-two . . . take away . . .

**Di**   No. Twenty take away nine.

**Rose**   Is it?

**Di**   Yes.

**Rose**   Why's that?

**Di**   You want to take how old you were from how old you are to get how long ago it happened, which is eleven.

**Rose**   Oh yes.

**Di**   And your mum's fifty-two now.

**Rose**   Yes.

**Di**   So she was forty-one.

**Rose**   Yes, brilliant, fifty-two take away eleven is forty-one, so she was forty-one when he died, yes.

**Di**   So she had a lot of life in front of her – has a lot of life in front of her now, but –

**Rose**   But it's over.

**Di**   Yeah.

**Rose**   But you know what's even more amazing? The thing that stopped her living her life is a normal thing. I mean, death is awful, but it's normal.

*Dissolve to:*

**Viv**   You wouldn't have to tell your tutors the real story. You could make something up.

**Di**   Tell me anything that doesn't involve parents and doctors and a million questions. I don't even want to defer. I should leave this year, with my degree, which I won't manage unless I do some work and I can't. I'm fucked.

**Viv**   My mother was top of her class. There was no question of her going to uni. I'm having an education she was excluded from. I'll be able to get jobs she was excluded from. Earn wages she was excluded from. All of which really pisses my mother off. *Her* mother would have been a maid to someone like Rose, not friends with her. By sheer fluke of timing, we've landed plumb in the middle of a shift, and I intend to take my step up. We've got to get the benefit, Di. What we do now stretches miles ahead. We've got to work.

**Di**   Don't preach at me. You and Rose keep trying to take over. Stop trying to take me over.

*She buries herself under the covers, deep in the den.*

*Dissolve to:*

**Viv** *enters.* **Rose** *emerges smartly from the kitchen.*

**Rose**   Can you make me a corset?

**Viv**   What?

**Rose**   You told me once about a tube of elastic that makes a woman's body a sort of smooth tube. You said you had patterns. Can you make me one of those?

**Viv**   Why?

**Rose**   Because I need to look as if I'm not having a baby.

**Viv**   You're having a baby?!

**Rose**   Yes, and I don't want Charlie and Mum to know until it's too late for them to tell me I can't. Which is five months.

**Viv**   You don't have to have it.

**Rose**   I'm going to.

**Viv**   You have every right not to.

**Rose**   I know my rights, thank you, and I know my wrongs and I'm having this little person I've begun to make because I had a hell of a time making her.

**Viv**   I thought you'd given up sex!

**Rose**   This must have been from sex before.

**Viv**   You told me you were careful! Safe!

**Rose**   Something must have gone wrong.

**Viv**   You've got to have an AIDS test!

**Rose**   I will.

**Viv**   God Almighty, Rose, there is a depressing inevitability to this which –

**Rose**  Don't get pompous! I hate you when you're pompous! I don't need you to tell me what to do, I know what to do, I just need you to help me do it.

**Viv** *looks at* **Rose**. **Viv** *goes to a cupboard. Rummages for cloth, scissors, pins and a pen.*

**Viv**  Who's the father?

**Rose**  I've narrowed it down to six.

**Viv** *kneels by* **Rose** *with her materials.*

**Viv**  Pull your top up. I need to wrap this round you.

**Rose** *pulls her top up, gripping it under her chin.* **Viv** *wraps the cloth around* **Rose** *from armpit to hip and begins to pin it into a tight tube.*

**Viv**  Hold that a sec.

**Rose**  This doesn't seem stretchy enough.

**Viv**  I'm making a toile. When I've worked out how to do it, I'll make it in stretchy stuff.

**Rose**  I see. It won't harm the baby, I don't think. It'll just be snug.

**Viv**  Have you told Di?

**Rose**  I don't want to.

**Viv**  Where is she?

**Rose**  She's gone to see Elaine at Rape Crisis. She ran there.

**Viv**  She *ran*?! It's miles.

**Rose**  I know. I think it's right not to tell her. She's got enough on her plate. You think I'm stupid, don't you?

**Viv**  I think you're an idiot *savant*. Do you know what that means?

**Rose**  Yes, and I think you're a silly bar of soap yourself.

**Viv**  Do you think you've got to endure this because Di's endured something?

**Rose**   No.

**Viv**   You'd have wanted this baby if Di hadn't been raped?

**Rose**   We'll never know, will we, because life without Di being raped is gone. She did some work this morning.

**Viv**   Did she?

**Rose**   More than I did.

**Viv**   Don't stop working, Rose. You'll need a degree in your back pocket, you know. If you do have this baby –

**Rose**   I am –

**Viv**   Right. But after. Later. You'll need it.

**Rose**   Oh Viv, I don't give a butcher's dog – what is it? Monkey's bum.

**Viv**   Tuppenny fuck.

**Rose**   I don't give a tuppenny butcher's monkey fuck about Giotto and Rothko and Manet and Monet and Van Dyck and Van Eyck and Bacon and Bosch and Klee and Chagall – actually I *love* Chagall – I've written two pages of my dissertation, who knows if there'll be more, I might just scrape through, but fuck it, fuck 'em, I'm having a baby!

**Viv**   Keep still.

**Rose**   I mean that's a hell of a project, isn't it? Having a baby.

*Front door slams, off.* **Rose** *and* **Viv** *freeze.* **Rose** *is trapped in her tube of cloth.* **Viv** *starts to unpin, fast.*

**Di** (*off*)   Hiya!

**Viv**   Shit.

**Rose**   Quick, quick, quick. Hi, Di! How did you get on?

**Di** *enters, sweaty, in running gear, carrying post. She's tired, but stronger somehow.*

**Di**   Fine. Ran there. Saw Elaine. Ran back. Knackered.

**Rose**  Well done! That's amazing!

**Di** *dumps the post down.*

**Di**  Post. Right. I'm gonna get clean, eat something and do some work. What are you doing?

**Rose**  Viv's making me a dress.

**Di**  Nice.

*She goes out.*

**Rose**  There and back! That's absolutely miles.

**Viv**  Yeah.

*She reaches for the post, shuffles through it. Stares at an envelope.*

Oh my God.

**Rose**  What?

**Viv**  It's from New York.

*She shows **Rose** the stamp on the back of the envelope.*

**Viv**  The Institute of Fashion and Design.

**Rose**  Wendy-May Fleeshman!

**Viv**  Nancy-May!

**Rose**  Open it!

**Viv** *opens it, begins to unfold it.*

**Di** *enters.*

**Di**  Rose. Are you pregnant?

**Rose**  No! I'm not pregnant!

**Di**  There's a pregnancy book in the bathroom.

**Rose**  I am pregnant. It's okay. I'm pleased. I'm going to have it.

**Di**  How long have you known?!

**Viv** *is in her own, dream-like state, reading her letter.*

**Rose**   Not long.

**Di**   Why didn't you tell me?

**Rose**   I was going to.

**Di**   You would have told me before. You would have told me instantly. Don't treat me as if I'm different. I'm not.

**Rose**   Sorry, Di.

**Viv**   Oh my God.

**Di** *and* **Rose** *look over at* **Viv***.*

**Di**   What? What is it?

**Viv**   It's a letter from Nancy-May Fleeshman.

**Rose**   Read it.

**Viv**   'Dear Vivien, Thank you for your kind appreciation of my work. Thank you too for sending me so much of yours over the past two years. You have unmistakable enthusiasm for your subject. However, I read a good many student papers so I know that enthusiasm is not so hard to come by. What impresses me about you is how you have developed. Your early work, while engaging, was somewhat tricksy in style and unevenly argued . . . '

*She flicks a momentary, baffled glance at* **Di** *and* **Rose***.*

**Viv**   'Recent work shows refined analytical rigour and leaner prose. Would you like to come and work with me? I can't offer you much money but we can help you with a place to live in the city. Let me know what you think. Good luck in your exams. Best wishes, Nancy-May Fleeshman.'

*She looks up, moved. The room is filled with wonder.*

**Rose**   Oh Viv.

**Di**   Have you just got exactly what you wanted? By working hard and wanting it? Exactly what you wanted?

**Viv**   Yes.

**Di**   And you're having a baby?

**Rose**    I am.

**Di**    Dismantle the den.

*Music plays.* **Di** *and* **Viv** *clear the den away, aware of the music.*


## Scene Eight

*July 1986. Mossbank is shipshape.* **Rose** *is cannily dressed – maybe a fifties trapeze top and narrow trousers.* **Di** *and* **Viv** *plump cushions. All three strive for brightness.* **Rose** *poses.*

**Rose**    Oh no, she's not pregnant. Not at all. Not from this angle. Not from this angle. Not even from this angle.

**Di**    You look good. Good work, Viv.

**Rose** *gives a flash of her midriff, smoothly encased in a long white elastic tube, grubby with daily wear.*

**Viv**    Thank you.

**Rose**    What if he notices the second he walks in?

**Viv**    He won't.

**Di**    He'll just think you look well. Do you need a hand with your bags?

**Rose**    No thanks. They're by the door. There's so much stuff.

**Di**    Will you tell him straight away?

**Rose**    I thought I'd wait till we're on the motorway. I thought I might try something like: 'Charlie, thanks ever so for the lift home. I've got some bad news and some news which I think is good news. The bad news is, I haven't got a degree. The other news is, I'm having a baby.' We've got a five-hour drive to thrash it out. I can always leap on to a grass verge. It'll be fine. I mean, I'm terrified but fuck it, it's my life.

**Viv**    It is.

**Rose**    And then once I'm home all I have to do is tell Mum.

*Silence.*

**Di**    Will you phone us tonight? Tell us how you get on.

**Rose**    Yes, and will you take lots and lots of pictures of yourselves in caps and gowns and holding scrolls?

**Di**    Yeah.

**Rose**    We've still got half an hour. More, probably. Charlie's always late. What shall we do?

**Di**    Let's just sit and chat.

*They sit. Silence.*

It's weird to think of other people living here next year.

**Viv**    I hate them already.

**Rose**    Can I say something? I just want to say. Sorry. Um. I just want to say that – these two years – living here with you two in Mossbank – have been the . . . Oh dear. Sorry.

**Viv**    Don't, Rose.

**Rose**    No I want to. I just want to say. I just want to say that I know we're not going to be in the same place any more but that doesn't mean –

*The front door bing-bongs.*

He's early! He's never early. Maybe it's not him.

*She goes to peep.*

Oh no, it is.

*The front door bing-bongs again.* **Rose** *goes, turns, consumed with anguish.*

**Rose**    I don't want to go!

*Blackout.*

# Act Two

## Scene One

*November 1986. An American phone tone rings out.* **Di** *and* **Viv***'s faces appear in discs of light, disembodied, like moons.*

**Viv** (*woken*)  Hello.

**Di**  Rose has had her twins!

**Viv**  Oh. Fantastic.

**Di**  Two boys.

**Viv**  Oh, that's fantastic. Is everyone okay?

**Di**  Yeah. They're all fine. They're Japanese!

**Viv**  They're not!

**Di**  Yeah. They're absolutely gorgeous. Tiny little things with this thick shock of black hair. They're absolutely gorgeous.

**Viv**  How's Charlie with that?

**Di**  Well, he's pissed off 'cause Rose never mentioned the Japanese lad when she went through the possibles 'cause she was trying to keep the numbers down.

**Viv**  Oh no!

**Di**  Rose couldn't care less though. She's totally over the moon. She's high as a kite.

**Viv**  What did she say it was like? She must have said it was like something.

**Di**  She did. She said it was like Conrad. In reverse. Twice.

*They both laugh heartily.*

**Viv**  Has she got an address for the Japanese lad?

**Di**  She's going to try and get one. When are you coming home?

**Viv**   I can't leave New York till after Christmas.

*Blackout.*


**Scene Two**

*February 1987. Marylebone Station. Sound of trains and the footsteps of people streaming by on the concourse.* **Di** *and* **Viv** *wait anxiously at a café table, looking about, stretch-necked.* **Viv***'s no longer dressed in clothes from another era but in chic black.*

**Viv**   There she is!

**Di**   Where?

**Viv**   There!

*They jump up and down waving big 'X's with their arms.* **Rose** *hurtles on, looking wild and careworn. She throws herself from one pair of arms to the other.*

**Rose**   Oh! Oh! Oh! Helloooooh! I'm so sorry! I didn't know what to do! What a disaster. It took ages! It's meant to be just over *one hour*! Something happened with the overhead line! They put us all on *buses*! And you *waited*! Oh Viv! Look at you!

**Viv**   Hello, Rose.

**Rose**   Oh, Di!

*She rubs the nape of* **Di***'s neck with gritted-teeth joy.*

**Rose**   Rrrrrr!

**Di** *accepts the attack with grace.*

**Rose**   So! Where shall we go?

**Di**   When?

**Rose**   For lunch! Now!

**Di**   We haven't got time.

**Rose**   Why? What's the time?

**Di**  Just gone two.

**Rose**  No! No! Look!

*She looks at her own watch.*

Twenty to one!

**Di**  I think you've stopped.

**Rose**  No! What do you make it?

**Viv**  Same. Two.

**Rose**  No! Two's when I've got to go! Two thirty-two's my train back!

**Di**  Get a later one!

**Rose**  I can't! I only left milk for – I fed them at ten. I left them milk for one o'clock. I thought I'd be back by half three-ish. They'll be starving. I can't wait either. I'm bursting already.

*She plaintively flashes open her coat and cardigan. Her T-shirt has two dark patches of leaked breast milk. She is terribly distressed.*

Oh God, I'm so stupid! I wanted to just have a little bit of time to myself with you two and see a tiny bit of London and I worked it out so carefully but I didn't think about anything going wrong!

**Di**  Have you definitely got to get that train?

**Rose**  Yes!

**Viv**  Okay. Well, that still gives us nearly half an hour.

**Rose**  *Half an hour is nothing!* What if the line's still broken on the way back?

**Di**  It won't be.

**Viv**  It's not your fault if it is.

**Di**  Shall I get you a tea?

**Rose**  No, don't go away for a second. Sit, sit, sit.

*They sit.*

Are these your crumbs?

**Viv**    Yeah.

**Rose**    I'll have these. Can I?

**Viv**    Course you can.

**Rose** *eats crumbs from* **Viv***'s plate, sips a leftover drink.*

**Rose**    You love New York, don't you, Viv? You love it. Tell me everything.

**Viv**    I want to know about you.

**Rose** *hasn't met with sympathy for some time. It floors her.*

**Rose**    Oh. I'm. I'm okay. I'm very very fucking tired. That's the trouble. And I don't like living at home, obviously, but, you know – that's my doing. Um. Mum's okay. She's – you know – still pretty dopey but she's okay with the boys. Charlie's horribly helpful. You know. Really thinks he knows how to do everything and really thinks I don't. And there's this woman from the village who comes sometimes and she's horrible. They just really disapprove. It's like a – *gas* of disapproval the whole time. Oh, I have sinned and I have fallen. Sometimes I wish they'd thrown me out. I think – you know – I think one day, when I'm not so totally tired – I might even like my boys. I'm so lonely. I do like them but it's like – what's the man with the boulder?

**Viv**    Sisyphus.

**Rose**    It's like Sisyphus. But two boulders. Crying ones. Oh God. Sorry. I've just got to put my head down. Just for a second.

*She rests her head on the table.*

Sorry.

**Di** *makes a cushion for* **Rose***, eases it under her head and rubs her back.* **Di** *and* **Viv** *look at each other across* **Rose***'s spent form. Stunned silence.*

**Di**    She's asleep. I felt her go.

**Viv**    The longed-for reunion. Two hours late and unconscious.

**Di**    Poor Rose.

**Viv**    She'll be all right.

**Di**    It's out of our league, isn't it?

**Viv**    Yeah, it is, it's – It's kind of shocking.

*They look about at the busy station.*

**Di**    Let's go back on the train with her. Let her sleep now, then go back with her.

**Viv**    And then what?

**Di**    Well. Come straight back.

**Viv**    Okay.

**Di**    'Cause she needs to sleep.

**Viv**    Yeah. Okay.

*Silence.*

People don't walk like this in New York.

**Di**    How do they walk?

**Viv**    Forward.

**Di**    What's this, then?

**Viv**    Downwards. They're all trying to go downstairs into a cellar. Look. They're all weighed down. Slumped.

**Di**    They look normal to me.

**Viv**    That's what's depressing. It does look normal till you get away.

**Di**    I need to get away.

**Viv**    Come and stay.

**Di**   I will. When I've got the money. Being back at home's doing my head in. I've gone backwards. I've gone back to fish on Fridays and not being a lesbian. Since you've started working, do you think about money differently?

**Viv**   In what way?

**Di**   Want it more.

**Viv**   Not really.

**Di**   I do. All the time I spend in that office, all the time I'm not free – which is *masses* of time – look, obviously, I'm not going to be paid much or do anything scintillating in my first job – but what I'm paid versus the time it takes away from me just *does not add up*. It would if I made enough money to change things. Buy my mum and dad's house for them. Buy Rose a nanny. Move out. It's kind of shocking. I really want to make money.

**Viv**   Set your mind to it, I'm sure you will.

**Di**   I don't think I like having a boss.

**Viv**   Be your own boss.

**Di**   Last Tuesday, it was exactly a year ago that I was –

**Viv**   I know. I thought about that. I thought about you.

**Di**   Exactly a year. So. Tuesday morning I was parking the car – well, Mrs Di's car, she lets me drive it to work – and there was this woman locking her car up and I thought, that looks like Elaine. It was. It was Elaine.

**Viv**   No way.

**Di**   She was going to a job interview. She's left Rape Crisis. She was literally in town for just that morning. It was uncanny. I said, you know, it's a year ago *today* and here we are, in a car park, in another town, doing different things and we bump into each other.

**Viv**   That is extraordinary.

**Di**   So we met up at lunchtime. It felt like a good thing to happen, you know, on that day.

**Viv**   Yeah.

**Di**   She's a good woman. We've spoken on the phone a couple of times. Mrs Di calls her my new friend Elaine. 'It's your new friend Elaine on the phone.' You really don't think about money?

**Viv**   I should, because I'm paid practically nothing, but the reason I don't, I think, is because I'm satisfied.

**Di**   With your job?

**Viv**   With everything.

**Di**   Wow.

**Viv**   Sometimes you need a brand-new city. Sometimes you've been propped up against the wrong background. I'm not any more.

**Di**   That's great.

**Viv**   I'm working with this seriously clever woman, who's put her faith in me, in this fascinating workplace in this *mettlesome* city. My clock ticks quicker there, my brain fires faster. I'm better there. Everything's better there.

**Di**   That's great.

**Viv**   Come.

**Di**   I will.

*Silence. She feels very lonely.*

I'd better get the train tickets.

**Viv**   Have some cash.

**Di**   Later. If I'm not back by twenty past, you should probably start waking her up.

**Viv**   Okay.

**Di** *goes.* **Viv** *adjusts her position so she can rest her hand on* **Rose***'s back as* **Di** *did.* **Viv** *strokes* **Rose** *with love and pride and looks out at all the people in the country she has left.*

*Blackout.*


### Scene Three

*May 1988. Little Kimble Station.* **Rose** *and* **Di** *stand on the single platform waiting for* **Di***'s train. It's a fine day and* **Rose** *is swinging her arms.* **Di** *has a rucksack.*

**Rose**    Thanks for coming, Di, thanks for coming to stay.

**Di**    It was fun. It was funny.

**Rose**    Will you come again?

**Di**    Definitely.

**Rose**    You weren't put off?

**Di**    No.

**Rose**    I don't know what to do with my arms any more!

*She holds them straight out.*

I'm always pushing a buggy!

*She tries hips, pockets, folding.*

What do people do? Honestly, I think I might have to keep pushing the buggy even when the boys don't need it. Put two little pigs in it and push it around.

**Di**    Just go straight on to a tartan shopping trolley. Skip the twenty years in the middle when you've got nothing to push.

**Rose**    Was the house like you expected?

**Di**    I expected a nutty set-up, from things you'd said.

**Rose**    Yes.

**Di**    But it is mental.

**Rose**   It's not a mess so much as just very, very *full*.

**Di**   Charlie found his glasses in the bread bin.

**Rose**   I know. The thing about the countryside is you can spread. You know, when there's newspapers and jam jars coming out of your ears you just put them in the porch, and when the porch is full you just put them in the shed, and when the shed is full you just build another one and before you know it you've got your own sort of personal village full of rubbish. And Charlie won't throw anything away and Mum doesn't move so it's only going to get worse, and what really annoys me is when they die – which I don't want to hurry up or anything and I'm not saying it's going to happen soon but, you know –

**Di**   Chances are.

**Rose**   Exactly, and when they do it'll be *Muggins* sorting out all the jam jars because Mum didn't take the precaution of having any other children, which I think was very selfish.

*A bell rings further down the platform.*

**Di**   Is that the train coming?

**Rose**   Yes. Will you come again?

**Di**   Yes.

*A car horn toots.*

That's Charlie. He toots me when they wake up.

**Di**   He can wait. He can wait two minutes. I'm going to ring Viv after work and tell her all about you.

**Rose**   She won't answer. She's always out. And when she does answer she's only ever got five minutes. Don't pick up the phone, then! If you're too busy and important! And she says '*on* the weekend'.

**Di**   I had to give her some stick about '*semester*'.

**Rose**   Honestly, it's such a pose. Viv's such a poser.

**Di**   I don't think she's having a ball at all. I think she's sat there shivering in front of one bar on the fire, with her coat on, eating marrowfat peas from the tin. Rats crawling around. Nancy-May Fleeshman's a bitch –

**Rose**   Nancy-May Fleeshman fired her –

**Di**   Nancy-May Fleeshman never existed. Viv wrote to herself. Yeah, so she's sat there in some little armpit of a flat, not even in New York, not answering the phone, apart from every couple of months when she picks it up – flicks the rats off it and picks it up – and tells us she's never been so culturally stimulated in her life.

*They laugh. The approaching train can be heard.*

**Rose**   I hope I pass my driving test. I'll get in Charlie's car, just with the boys, just the three of us, drive to the sea.

**Di**   Excellent.

*The car horn toots again, testily.*

**Rose**   My driving teacher wants me. Mr Cooper.

**Di**   I hope he's not gonna get you.

**Rose**   No, he's quite unpleasant but the way he looks at me gives me the fanny gallops.

**Di**   How does he look at you?

**Rose**   Like he's a dog and I'm a chop.

**Di**   Don't give Mr Cooper what he wants.

**Rose**   That's all very well for you to say, Di, you're getting it. You and Elaine are getting lots of it. I'm doing an awful lot of holding and an awful lot of feeding and I would like to be held, by someone with bigger hands than me.

**Di**   Mr Cooper's a bum steer. You need to get on your own two feet. Spend your energy on that.

**Rose**   I can't get on my own two feet till they go to nursery!

**Di**   Get ready for that, then! You need to get out of there before you forget how to do things your own way! Get your own car!

**Rose**  How the hell am I supposed to do that?!

*They are drowned out by the train.*

*Blackout.*


## Scene Four

*April 1998. Phone rings out, is picked up.* **Di** *and* **Rose** *like moons.*

**Di**  Hello?

**Rose**  Have you got it?!

**Di**  Hello Rose. Have I got what?

**Rose**  Are you at home?

**Di**  No. Work.

**Rose**  Is Elaine at home?

**Di**  No, she's at work with me. We're just in.

**Rose**  What time does your post come?

**Di**  About ten usually. Why?

**Rose**  Big secret.

**Di**  Am I going to get something in the post?

**Rose**  I think so!

**Di**  Is it from you?

**Rose**  Noooooooo.

**Di**  Is it from Viv?

**Rose**  Yes!

**Di**  What is it?

**Rose**  I shouldn't tell you.

**Di**  Rose. Tell me. You want to.

**Rose**   I was hoping you'd put up a bit of a fight.

**Di**   Rose. Please don't tell me what I'm going to get in the post. I'd much prefer to wait all day wondering what it is.

**Rose**   I'm sorry, Di, but I'm going to tell you because I can't contain myself.

**Di**   Hhhh. Okay. If you insist. What is it?

**Rose**   *A return ticket to New York!*

**Di**   You're kidding.

**Rose**   And an invitation to a *gala ball* in *June* at *Viv's work* and a note from her saying she hopes we can both come – for a week – and it's her treat and Di – the ticket – well, it's a voucher to be redeemed thing but it's . . . BUSINESS CLASS!

*Fantastic music.*


**Scene Five**

*June 1998. New York. Night.* **Viv**'s *apartment.* **Di** *and* **Viv** *and* **Rose** *are fresh back from the Gala. In evidence are the spoils of party: goody bags, helium balloons, flowers.* **Di** *and* **Viv** *and* **Rose** *are dressed in their own versions of finery.* **Rose** *is kicking off her shoes.* **Di** *is mucking about with balloons (maybe biffing one tied to a chair).* **Viv**, *wired, is pouring and handing out champagne.*

**Viv**   Let's drink . . . to the fact . . . that I didn't . . . fuck it up.

**Rose**   Of course you didn't!

**Viv**   Thank *fuck* that's over.

**Rose**   Didn't you enjoy it?

**Viv**   No! Too nervous.

**Rose**   You didn't seem it!

**Viv**   Good.

**Di**   It went down a storm, didn't it?

**Viv**   Nancy-May Fleeshman was very good at the gala. All eyes were on me tonight, including hers. What would I do differently? Would the speeches be good?

**Di**   Your speech was great.

**Viv**   You don't want to fuck up in that room. That is a very heavy room. If you fucked up there, you wouldn't have to fuck up anywhere else. You'd have covered it.

**Rose**   You didn't fuck up.

**Viv**   *Everyone* was in that room.

**Rose**   I know we were.

**Viv**   And how much did we raise? We won't know that for a while.

**Di**   It went down a storm. Enjoy it.

**Viv**   I know. I will.

**Di**   Did you hear about my *cultural faux pas*?

**Viv**   No.

**Rose**   Has anyone seen my goody bag?

**Di**   You had it when we came in.

**Viv**   What happened?

**Di**   The guy with the beard. Queer. Ted?

**Viv**   Ted. Yeah.

**Rose** *hunts in their pile of coats/wraps for her goody bag as:*

**Rose**   I had a sexy dance with Ted.

**Viv**   He's a fabulous dancer.

**Rose**   Gay men are fabulous dancers.

**Viv**   You can't say that.

**Di**   I practically gave him a heart attack.

**Rose**   Here it is!

**Viv**    *How?*

**Di**    I was sat next to him. Do you want mine, Rose? So the boys can have one each?

**Rose**    Don't you want to give yours to Elaine? Give it to Elaine.

**Viv**    What happened with Ted?

**Di**    After all the speeches – we'd been stuck at the table for ages and the waiters were coming round with brandy – I said to Ted, 'You know what? I *could murder a fag.*' We sorted it out, but it was touch and go.

*The apartment phone rings.* **Viv** *answers.*

**Viv**    Hello? – Hi, honey! –

**Rose** *and* **Di** *spin to look at each other in delighted amazement.*

**Viv**    No, we just got back – Did you? – *Did* she? – That's great. – No, we're just having a nightcap. – I will. – Okay. That sounds great. I'll call you in the morning. – Bye, honey.

**Rose** *and* **Di** *look at each other in even greater delighted amazement.*

**Viv**    Ted says you're both adorable and he'd like to take us out for brunch tomorrow –

**Rose**    'Hi honey', 'Bye honey'?! –

**Viv**    – and Nancy-May Fleeshman was delighted with the gala.

**Rose**    *Viv!* 'Hi honey', 'Bye honey'?! –

**Viv**    What?! He's a friend!

**Rose**    But Viv, honey, we've never heard you call anyone honey. Have we, honey?

**Di**    No, honey.

**Viv**    Well, get with the programme.

**Viv** *sweeps out with the champagne bottle and the flowers.* **Di** *gazes out of a window at the city below.* **Rose** *sits, gazing at her own bare feet.*

**Rose**   Oh Rose, whose toes are those? Viv!

**Viv** (*off*)   Yeah?

**Rose**   Thank you for my pedicure!

**Viv** (*off*)   You're welcome!

**Rose**   You should have had one, Di, it was wonderful.

**Di**   I don't like people fiddling with my feet.

**Rose**   Not even Elaine?

**Di**   No, she's allowed. Rose. Come and see.

**Rose** *goes and joins* **Di** *at the window. They stare down together, awestruck.*

**Di**   Gorgeous, gorgeous city.

**Rose**   That's what Viv sees every day.

*An extraordinary thought.* **Viv** *enters with the champagne bottle in an ice bucket. She cuts a startlingly glamorous figure – relaxed now.*

**Rose**   Viv. Your life is like an arrow. You aimed true and you shot straight and you went bang into the bullseye of what you planned.

**Viv**   That's a highly romanticised and partisan version of events, Rose.

**Di**   It is a blast to see you in your realm. I feel proud.

**Rose**   Me too. Proud as a lupin.

**Viv**   I'm glad you're here.

**Rose**   I do worry about the bottles of green stuff in your fridge –

**Viv**   Wheatgrass –

**Rose**   So you say. And I worry about all the black clothes in your wardrobe –

**Viv**   If you're serious about cut, you must sacrifice colour –

**Di**   But you're pompous as ever so life is good –

**Rose**   But *everything* black? No concessions?

**Viv**   Tampax and toothpaste.

**Rose**   I'm going to put this in my suitcase so I don't forget it.
Life *is* good.

*She pads off with her goody bag.* **Viv** *and* **Di** *stare out of the window*
*together.* **Viv** *slings an easy arm around* **Di**.

**Viv**   Life *is* good.

**Rose** (*off*)   Can we go back to that ice-cream place
tomorrow?

**Viv**   Yes.

**Rose** (*off*)   And the Goo-goo-goo-goo –

**Viv**   Guggenheim. Yes.

**Di**   I'd like to run in the park.

**Rose** *reappears wearing an enormous* 'I ❤ *NY' shirt, holding a photo.*

**Rose**   I found that photo.

*She shows it to* **Viv**.

**Viv**   God, they're getting tall, Rose.

**Rose**   I know. Gregory's taller. Can you see? Cary's going to
be broader, I think.

**Viv**   Charlie's looking old.

**Rose**   Well, he is. Sixty now.

**Viv**   That's why there's a big 'SIXTY' on that cake.

**Rose**   I made that cake.

**Di**   Show her Patrice.

**Rose**   That's Patrice.

**Viv**   Nice. Where's your mum?

**Rose**  Indoors.

**Di**  Pass it. Let's get a proper look at these boys.

**Viv** *passes the photo.*

**Di**  Ahh. Nearly as nice as my dogs. Who wants to see my dogs?

**Rose**  Me.

**Di** *dips into her pocket and produces a little photo wallet.*

**Viv**  That is weird.

**Di**  What?

**Viv**  Being able to produce a picture of your dogs that fast.

**Di**  That's Gloria, sitting on Elaine. And that's Sprout, looking a bit hot. What would you rather have, Viv? Those gangly things with black hair or these little cuties?

**Viv** *looks from* **Di***'s photo to* **Rose***'s.*

**Viv**  I couldn't possibly say.

**Rose**  Charlie sold Mossbank.

**Viv** *and* **Di**  No!

**Rose**  He made fifty thousand pounds.

**Di**  That was a great house.

**Rose**  It was.

*They put their photos away and think of Mossbank, good and bad.*

**Rose**  Do you think I should get married? Patrice keeps asking and I keep saying no.

**Di**  Why?

**Rose**  Because it's square.

**Di**  Marrying an Algerian gardener isn't square, not for a single mum with Japanese twins.

**Rose**   No, *I'm* not and *he* isn't but *it* is. What do you think, Viv?

**Viv**   Di says he's great.

**Rose**   He is. But why does anyone need to get married?

**Viv**   They don't.

**Rose**   I *clawed* my way through their babyhood. They survived the village school. They made friends. I got myself a cooking job. We got out. Charlie and Mum expected us to come snivelling back and we didn't. We made it. *All alone.* So it sticks like a fishbone to get married.

**Viv**   It negates what you've done.

**Rose**   Yes.

**Di**   What she's done is in the bag.

**Rose**   I thought you'd think it was a terrible idea.

**Di**   It would be terrible if you wanted to and didn't 'cause you thought you were letting the side down.

**Rose**   I would be.

**Viv**   What's he like?

**Rose**   He isn't like anything. He's just the one.

**Viv** *nods, impressed somehow.*

**Di**   If queers could marry, I'd marry Elaine.

**Rose**   Maybe I'll do it.

**Di**   Well. I'm going to stake out my side of the bed before you come in and start flailing around.

**Rose**   Okay. If I got married, would you come?

**Di** *and* **Viv**   Yes!

**Rose**   Would you be my best women?

**Di** *and* **Viv**   Yes.

**Rose**    Would you say a few words?

**Di** *and* **Viv**    Yes.

**Rose**    Okay. I'll think about it.

**Di**    Goodnight, my friends.

**Rose**    Night.

**Viv**    Night.

**Di** *goes.*

**Rose**    The thing about this T-shirt, Viv, is it's actually true.

**Viv**    You look just the same, Rose.

**Rose**    I don't look just the same but I feel just the same and if you feel just the same way about me, that'll do. You're tired.

**Viv**    I suddenly am.

**Rose**    Go to bed. Can I ring home?

**Viv**    Course.

**Rose**    They'll just be waking up.

**Viv**    Do they like Patrice?

**Rose**    They love him.

**Viv**    Do they still ask about Kimihiko?

**Rose**    Oh yes.

**Viv**    What do you say?

**Rose**    I just always say the facts. We were very young. It was a lovely night. I tried to find him. I don't know if he wants to be found. And that we'll go to Japan when they're sixteen, so we can see it. They don't *seem* to be horrified. Viv, you're falling asleep in front of my eyes. Go to bed.

**Viv**    Okay.

*She hauls herself upright.*

**Rose**    Goodnight.

**Viv**    Goodnight, honey.

*She goes.* **Rose** *gets the phone and sits with it in her lap. She looks at her watch. She picks up the receiver and carefully dials the international code and her own number. She waits. Her face lights up.*

**Rose**    Good morning.

*Blackout.*


## Scene Six

*April 1999.* **Di** *stands in afternoon light at a lectern. She holds index cards with notes on them.*

**Di**    When Rose asked me to speak at her wedding I was really pleased, and I was nervous, because I wanted to get it right. I wrote it and rewrote it and I did it to Viv over the phone and she said it was ready. And then Rose died. It turns out that what you need to say at someone's funeral isn't so different from what you want to say at their wedding.

I met Rose sixteen years ago at university. That's when Rose chose me and Viv and we chose her. We set up home at 42 Mossbank Road, thanks to Charlie. Thank you, Charlie. Rose made life look so easy. She enjoyed so many things you could think it was an act. It wasn't. She had appetite. Rose loved men. That's something often said with a sting in the tail: 'She loved too many men. She loved indiscriminately. She didn't love women.'

No one who's stood by a market stall in the snow while Rose chooses oranges could call her indiscriminate. Me and Viv are women and she was soppy about us. Once. When I was ill. She fed me.

Gregory and Cary, you should know, while your mum prepared for you to be born, aged nineteen, she was the most determined I've ever seen anyone be. Patrice, Rose was rock-solidly happy these last few years when you came to live with her and the boys.

I used to think growing up together meant you just happened
to shoot upwards alongside certain people but now I think the
way you shoot up – the shape you shoot up in – is contingent
on a few people shooting up with you. If something bad or
sad or good happens to one of you, it almost happens to the
other. If you have a friend you grew up with like that, like
this, you believe the arrangement's for life, and when they pull
out – even though you know it's by accident – because they
stepped off the pavement without looking – what you feel is
sadder than I knew was possible. Me and Viv will have to
continue growing up without Rose. It won't be as good.

*Blackout.*

## Scene Seven

*Behind the church hall.* **Viv** *is slumped in a corner, turned away.* **Di**
*appears, looking for* **Viv***. It takes her a while to see* **Viv** *in the gloom.*
**Di** *holds a bottle of beer and a box. She sets the box down.*

**Di**    Viv? Viv. Wake up.

**Viv**    I'm not asleep.

**Di**    What are you doing out here?

**Viv**    I couldn't stand it.

**Di** *squats down beside* **Viv***.*

**Di**    Can you sit up?

**Viv**    What kind of world is this?

**Di** *rests her hand on* **Viv***'s back. She checks her watch.*

**Di**    We need to go.

**Viv** *sits up. She is cradling an empty wine bottle.*

**Viv**    I couldn't listen to those people. Who were they talking
about? What were we doing in a church? It wasn't even a
decent church. It was a conservatory with candlesticks.

Everyone talking shit apart from you, and then everyone trooping back to *another* hideous building to jostle for sausage rolls. And those boys. In their chinos. Laughing. Did you see them? With their friends. Looking at girls. At their mother's funeral.

**Di**    They're fourteen. It's too much.

**Viv**    It's offensive.

**Di**    It's too big for them. It's hardly happening to them.

**Viv**    Well, it's happening to me.

**Di**    I know. Viv, we need to go. I need to go.

**Viv**    In their fucking chinos. Don't you think it's offensive?

**Di**    No.

**Viv**    It is. Will you get me a drink?

**Di**    No.

**Viv**    Those hair-sprayed bitches. Swarming round the mother of the corpse. Did you see them? Actively aroused.

**Di**    We need to go, love.

**Viv**    No one except us should be allowed to talk about Rose. She's ours.

**Di**    She's lots of people's. Come on, you're freezing.

**Viv**    Yes, I am. And I've pissed in the bushes as well.

**Di**    Let's get you in the car.

**Viv**    *I don't want to get in the car!*

**Di**    You've got to help me here, Viv.

**Viv**    No, you've got to help me.

**Di**, *frustrated, pissed off, sets the beer down, removes her jacket and puts it round* **Viv**'s *shivering shoulders.* **Di** *hauls* **Viv** *up.*

**Viv**    You're the man, I'm the woman.

**Di**  Okay.

**Viv**  The man should give the woman his beer.

**Di**  No.

**Viv** *reaches for the beer.* **Di** *tries to stop her.* **Viv** *snatches the bottle, spilling and wasting the last few drops.* **Viv** *hurls the bottle away with a roaring cry. Sound of it smashing. She hurls the empty wine bottle off too, with another roaring cry. Sound of it smashing.*

**Viv**  We need to tell them they're all liars – with no taste! Come on! Let's tell them! Charlie in particular has it coming. 'Charlie, you eulogising revisionist, you made Rose's life a misery. You conducted a campaign of punishment that nearly killed her and now she's dead she's perfect. Charlie: you are a cunt.'

**Di**  She loved him.

**Viv**  And the mother. She's a cunt. I would pity the mother if I thought the pain and shame and horror and shame at herself would hit, but thanks to being sedated round the clock she's off scot free. Just *with it* enough to organise an insult dressed up as a travesty dressed up as a funeral. Let's tell her!

**Di**  I need to go.

**Viv**  Come on!

**Di**  No.

**Viv**  When did you get so wimpy?

*She starts swiping at* **Di**.

**Viv**  When did you get so wet?

*She keeps swiping at* **Di**.

**Viv**  Why won't you fight for her?

**Di**  I need to get out of here.

**Viv**  Come back in and fight with me! Fight!

**Di** *bats* **Viv** *away.*

**Di**    You have to catch your plane! I have to get back to
Mrs Di!

**Viv**    My plane's not till six o'clock tomorrow morning!

**Di**    You have to catch the train to make the plane.

**Viv**    They can have the AGM without me.

**Di**    Mum can't go into hospital without me. Help me, Viv.
Your last train's in forty minutes. I'll come to New York as
soon as Mrs Di's on the mend. We'll go to all the places we
went with Rose. Yeah?

**Viv**    Yeah.

**Di**    We'll celebrate her. We'll make a ceremony. That's what
we need to do. I need to.

**Viv** *makes a small ball of herself, hugging her knees, face buried.*

**Viv**    I'm not going back to New York.

**Di**    You'll be better once you get there.

**Viv**    I'm not going.

**Di** *looks at balled-up* **Viv**. *She looks at her watch.* **Di** *almost weeps
with lonely frustration. She summons all her patience. She fetches the box.
She sets it in front of* **Viv**.

**Di**    Look in there.

**Viv** *opens the box. She unpacks a scarf, a bicycle pump. She recognises
them immediately. She looks at* **Di**.

**Di**    Charlie found it. She saved it all.

**Viv** *takes out some battered papers.*

**Viv**    My writing. I wrote this.

**Viv** *unpacks the Rose bowls.*

**Di**    Would you like to take it? To New York?

**Viv**    Don't you want it?

**Di**    We shouldn't split it up.

**Viv**   No.

**Di**   You have it for a bit. Then, when I come and see you, I'll bring it home for a bit.

**Viv**   Yes.

**Di**   Okay, love. So why don't you take it with you to the car and I'll fetch your things and say goodbye. Okay?

**Viv**   Okay.

**Di** *hands* **Viv** *her car keys.*

**Di**   I'll just say a quick bye-bye and I'll be out.

**Viv** *is re-packing the box, pacified.*

**Di**   Mind yourself on the path. Someone's smashed some bottles.

**Viv**   Village vandals.

**Di** *heads off towards the hall.*

**Di**   Yeah.

**Viv** *heads off towards the car.*

*Blackout.*


## Scene Eight

*A phone rings out.* **Di** *picks up, just woken. Faces as moons.*

**Di**   Hello?

**Viv**   It's Viv.

**Di**   Where are you?

**Viv**   At the airport.

**Di**   Did you miss your flight?

**Viv**   No, I'm about to board. I lost the box.

**Di**   What?

**Viv**   I lost the box from Mossbank.

*In the silence, we hear* **Di***'s breath.*

**Viv**   I left it on the train. I realised when I got to the hotel. I went back to the station in a cab. They said nothing had been handed in. The train had been cleaned. It must have looked like rubbish.

**Di**   Did you drink on the train?

**Viv**   There was a trolley.

**Di**   Are you drunk now?

**Viv**   I haven't really been to sleep.

**Di**   There's no point talking if you're still drunk.

**Viv**   I'm not.

**Di**   Did you ask to look through the rubbish?

**Viv**   They wouldn't let me. The rubbish had gone. How could anyone think it was rubbish? How much brain does it take to see the difference between rubbish and . . .

**Di** *breathes for a while. Then silence.*

**Viv**   Are you there?

**Di**   Just about.

**Viv**   If you left something on a train in the States somebody would put it somewhere safe. Make a log of it. Log it, you know. And even if they'd mistaken it for trash, you'd get it back. You definitely would. This country's useless.

**Di**   I persuaded Elaine not to come yesterday. I said to her, 'This is something I have to do with Viv.' I thought we'd get through it together but you opted out by drinking. You left me, but I put up with it. I propped you up. I poured you on the train. I trusted you with the box from Mossbank.

**Viv**   It's only things.

*Arctic silence.*

**Viv**    Maybe it's too soon to say it but it's true. You only gave me the box to fob me off and get me in the car like a baby.

**Di**    I'm going to put the phone down now. When you can be wrong, and sorry, call me. I won't be calling you.

*The phone clicks. The line goes dead.*

**Di** *and* **Viv** *stare out.*

*Blackout.*

## Scene Nine

*August 2010. A hill.* **Viv** *waits.* **Di** *scoots up on a disability scooter.* **Viv***, surprised and moved, embraces* **Di***.* **Di** *stays on her scooter, only releasing one hand to receive* **Viv***'s embrace.*

**Viv**    You look better than I expected.

**Di**    I'm fine.

**Viv**    Charlie said you were bad.

**Di**    Charlie always lays it on thick. What happened to head-to-toe black?

**Viv**    I came to think it affected.

**Di**    It was.

**Viv**    Charlie said it came back.

**Di**    They said it might, when they got rid of the first one. The second one was tiny, lower down. They cut it out. Everyone's confident that's it.

**Viv**    That's wonderful. How's Elaine?

**Di**    Fat.

**Viv**    The dogs?

**Di**    Dead.

**Viv**   You're covered in dog hair.

**Di**   We got new dogs.

**Viv**   How's business?

**Di**   We sold the domain name.

**Viv**   Wow. Tell me more.

**Di**   That's it.

**Viv**   I can't picture Elaine fat.

**Di**   A little thicker. Aren't we all? You don't seem to be, actually. Very Viv.

**Viv**   What's wrong?

**Di**   You crossed the Atlantic because you thought I was dying.

**Viv**   Yes.

**Di**   I'm not.

**Viv**   I'm overjoyed you're not.

**Di**   I didn't need you to.

**Viv**   I needed to.

**Di**   Did you now.

**Viv**   Have I done something wrong?

**Di**   Says it all, doesn't it?

**Viv**   What?

**Di**   We never used to need a crisis. I can't be doing with things that don't work any more, Viv. Sorry. Life's too short.

**Viv**   What have I done?

**Di**   We never really got back on track. We've limped along and it's no one's fault but we're flogging a dead horse.

**Viv**   Tell me what I've done.

**Di**   It's no one's fault.

**Viv**   What then?

**Di**   Are you nervous when we meet up?

**Viv**   No.

**Di**   You don't think, before, 'I hope this goes okay?' You don't feel relieved when it does?

**Viv**   But it does.

**Di**   You don't feel the things that aren't said? Just off?

**Viv**   Sometimes.

**Di**   We've been just off for years. So let's admit it and call it a day and have one less thing in life that isn't true.

*Silence.*

**Viv**   You've arranged to meet me on a hill to chuck me for some reason. So you'd better tell me what I've done.

**Di**   We're on a hill because Elaine won't have you in the house.

**Viv**   What have I done to Elaine?!

**Di**   She doesn't think you're a friend to me.

**Viv**   What do you think?

**Di**   I think you don't know how to. You appear to be a friend, for a while, and then you say something or do something and the floor goes from under me and I think, 'Fuck – I'm on my own here.'

**Viv**   You'll have to give me an example.

**Di**   This won't work, Viv, because you'll have to put yourself in my shoes and that's the bit you can't do.

**Viv**   Give me an example.

**Di**   Okay. Bear with me 'cause this is an old one but it's – it says it all. The year after I was raped – on the anniversary –

you told me later that you'd thought about it on the day, thought about me. But you didn't phone me. That's the bit that would have done me good. Your thought, in your head, about me, is no use to me.

**Viv**   Give me another example.

**Di**   After Rose died.

**Viv**   Have you got any examples from this century?

**Di**   That's right. Bat it away.

**Viv**   When I think about the funeral I feel sick. You know that.

**Di**   I mean after.

**Viv**   The phone call – after – plays back when I can't sleep. When I said – about the things she'd saved from Mossbank - which were far more than things because Mossbank's where we were made – and I said they were 'just things' – that makes me burn.

**Di**   That doesn't bother me.

**Viv**   Are you serious?

**Di**   Genuinely doesn't bother me in the slightest any more. You fucked up, you know, you were a mess, of course you were, you got drunk, you lost the box, you handled it terribly. It wasn't aimed at me. But you never asked me over. We said I'd come to New York. I needed to blow. I needed to rant and wail, like you, with you, maybe while you looked after me maybe, but that never happened. You never asked me.

**Viv**   I didn't know. You didn't say.

**Di**   I shouldn't have to say! I shouldn't have to! A friend shouldn't have to spell it out. The other friend should get it.

**Viv**   I did ask you. You did come.

**Di**   Months later. Too late.

**Viv**   Well, I think it's too late to punish me for it.

*Silence.*

I'm sorry I was selfish.

**Di**    That is what you are, Viv.

**Viv**    I'm sorry I was thoughtless. I'm sorry I hurt you.

**Di**    I need to look after myself.

*Silence.* **Viv** *gets out a hip flask. She offers it to* **Di**. **Di** *declines.*

**Viv**    How's Mrs Di?

**Di**    In Mumbai. With the choir. She's been globetrotting since Dad died. Two new knees. One new hip.

**Viv**    God.

**Di**    I'm going to head off now.

**Viv**    Wouldn't it have been friendly of you to tell me what you needed, at the time? Isn't it unfriendly to resent my failure to guess correctly?

**Di**    I have to take my medication.

**Viv**    Isn't it good there's bits of each other that are alien? Isn't that right?

**Di**    I have to take it with food, so –

**Viv**    We have joint custody of a chunk of the past. If you chuck me, when you feel like going back there – and you will – you'll have to go alone. And so will I.

**Di**    The past is a waste of time.

**Viv**    I know! I've jettisoned great swathes of it, e.g. my parents. But I also know, now, that I need to be able to look across a room and find someone who gets it – doesn't just get right here right now but gets the lot, the whole long trail of everything that went before. Don't you?

**Di**    I get that with Elaine.

**Viv**    Okay. Okay. Begging's not my weapon of choice, so –

**Di**    Ta-ra.

**Viv**    This is a pretty shitty fucking stunt to pull, you know?
I don't accept this version of events. This version of me. Who
put the boys through university so they didn't have loans and
didn't bankrupt Patrice? Who flew them out to Long Island
every summer? What does that tell you?

**Di**    That you did good deeds. I know you did lots – I know
you did – but now you're going on about it, to look good. Not
so good.

**Viv**    I didn't do it to look good!

**Di**    Not even partly?

**Viv**    Of course partly! Have you – has anyone – ever, ever
done anything for one pure reason? Ever? Get real. I know
I turn to metal sometimes, when things are too big for me, or
I need to win, I know that! I can't stop it completely but I do
it less and less and I take the consequences and I know that
I do it! You stew on me for eleven years while I bust a gut to
do the right thing and you wait till now, when you think
you're untouchable, to bayonet me. That's expedient. It's
dishonest. I don't care how many lumps you've had cut off
your spine, this is low.

**Di**    Fuck you.

**Viv**    And you.

**Di** *scoots off.* **Viv** *drinks.*

**Viv**    I'm getting a divorce!

I got married!

To Ted the Poof!

*Eventually,* **Di** *reappears on her scooter. She stops, at a distance.*

**Viv**    It turned out he was gay.

**Di**    When did you get married?

**Viv**    Four months ago.

**Di**    You never said a word.

**Viv**    I know. Interesting, isn't it? I was happily married for a month and a half and then Ted fell in love with a boy.

**Di**    No shit.

**Viv**    The boy was new in town. He was adopted by that set you saw in action at the gala all those years ago. That small but mighty academic-museum-gallery set. Ted fell in love and moved out in a month. Everybody knew. Everyone saw it coming. When I say I was embarrassed, I mean embarrassed from the Hudson to the East River. Embarrassed from Canada to Florida. I am embarrassed twice round the equator. I've only recently been able to drag myself out of bed, I've been so embarrassed. I'm leaving New York I'm so embarrassed.

**Di**    Because of what people will think?

**Viv**    What they do think!

**Di**    You never used to need approval.

**Viv**    Of course I did. I had to cross the world for stranger approval. Have to write books for critical approval. Can't get enough approval down my gaping throat.

**Di**    I read your book.

**Viv**    And?

**Di**    It's the best book on gloves I've ever read.

*She takes the flask, has a good slug.*

You knew Ted was gay.

**Viv**    Yes.

**Di**    And you married him.

**Viv**    Yes.

**Di**    I don't get it.

**Viv**   Because you never saw me lose my head for a person.
Which I did, spectacularly, with him. I slept with people in
New York. I could do it there.

**Di**   Women? I always wondered.

**Viv**   No. Where's the holiday in that?

**Di**   All over the place.

**Viv**   The miracle is otherness.

**Di**   Not in my book. Not in Ted's.

**Viv**   I'm weird. I lie on the beach behind my sunglasses
mentally dressing people. I'm not that interested in sex, the
last taboo standing. But I was drugged by the beauty of Ted.

**Di**   Are we talking about the same Ted?

**Viv**   I used to watch him in the bath through a gap in the
door. I couldn't stop looking at him.

**Di**   *Ted?*

**Viv**   The elegance of him.

**Di**   He's a gay man.

**Viv**   I was Titania. We were incredibly close by the time we
got married. We'd been going around together for years – clubs,
bars, restaurants, trips away – we were seamless together –

**Di**   He's a gay man –

**Viv**   So when it came to him proposing and me accepting
and us planning it and going off to Mexico to do it – in all
that time – and in all the time we were married –

**Di**   – the entire fortnight –

**Viv**   – because we had such understanding – because we
were so in tune – because we were so enlightened about
sexuality and labels and boxes – because of all of that –

**Viv** *laughs.*

**Di**   What?

**Viv**    We –

*She laughs.*

**Di**    What?

**Viv**    We never –

*She just can't get it out. Every time she goes to make the sentence she is struck afresh by the absurdity. She is out of control.* **Di** *begins to submit to the laughing gas.*

**Di**    You never what?

**Viv**    We never actually mentioned the fact that it might be –

**Di**    Might be –

**Viv** (*mangled by laughter*)    A problem.

**Di**    Problem.

**Viv** (*crazy, laughing crescendo*)    We never actually mentioned the fact that it might be a problem for our marriage that he was gay!

**Di** *laughs at* **Viv** *laughing.* **Viv** *recovers.* **Di** *recovers.* **Di** *starts, setting* **Viv** *off. And so on. Eventually, drying laughed-out eyes:*

**Viv**    Ohh the folly. Ohhh the folly.

**Di**    You never mentioned it.

**Viv**    Never.

**Di**    You child.

**Viv**    I know.

*Silence.*

Do you ever see her these days?

**Di**    I saw her last week. Crossing the road.

**Viv**    I see her in New York. Bits of her. Her hair. Her walk. It's never her face.

**Di**    No.

**Viv**    I miss you.

**Di**    It's very hard.

**Viv**    It's worth the candle.

*Silence.*

**Di** *starts to hitch up her top.*

**Di**    Check it out.

*She reveals a white, surgical corset, fastened with Velcro straps.*

**Viv**    Oh it's not –

**Di**    It is.

**Viv**    It's not.

**Di**    It fucking is.

**Viv**    Holey Moley.

**Di**    I need to pop some pills and eat something. Got to. Sorry.

**Viv**    Okay.

**Di** *turns her scooter and scoots away. Just before she disappears:*

**Di**    Keep up.

**Viv** *hurries after* **Di***.*

*Blackout.*


## Scene Ten

*The empty space has, projected all over it, a vivid, full-scale image of Mossbank – apparently 3D, but flat. Music plays, fast and furious. It takes a moment to spot* **Di** *and* **Viv** *and* **Rose** *because the colours of the projection of Mossbank play all over them as they move, like animal print. For a brief blast, briefer than we want, we see the three of them, dancing for dear life.*